1964

# THE FRENCH NEW NOVEL

LAURENT LE SAGE

# THE FRENCH NEW NOVEL

## AN INTRODUCTION AND A SAMPLER

## LAURENT LE SAGE

THE PENNSYLVANIA STATE UNIVERSITY PRESS

UNIVERSITY PARK, PENNSYLVANIA          1962

# CONTENTS

ACKNOWLEDGMENTS

The author's thanks are hereby made to the following publishers for permission to use the materials indicated:

To Grove Press, Inc., for selections from *Molloy*, by Samuel Beckett (tr. by Patrick Bowles); *Malone Dies*, by Samuel Beckett (tr. by Mr. Beckett); *Ten-thirty on a Summer Night*, by Marguerite Duras (tr. by Anne Borchardt) and *Moderato Cantabile*, by Mme. Duras (tr. by Richard Seavers); *Monsieur Levert*, by Robert Pinget (tr. by Richard Howard); *The Voyeur, Jealousy*, and *The Erasers*, by Alain Robbe-Grillet (tr. by Richard Howard).

To G. P. Putnam's Sons for the quote from *Foreign Bodies*, by Jean Cayrol (tr. by Richard Howard).

To Simon and Schuster, Inc., for selections from Michel Butor's *Passing Time* and *A Change of Heart* (tr. by Jean Stewart) and *Degrees* (tr. by Richard Howard).

To George Braziller, Inc., for materials quoted from *Portrait of a Man Unknown* and *The Planetarium*, by Nathalie Sarraute (tr. by Maria Jolas); *The Grass, The Wind*, and *The Flanders Road*, by Claude Simon (tr. by Richard Howard); *Nedjma*, by Kateb Yacine (tr. by Richard Howard).

To Librairie Gallimard for extracts from *La Tour*, by Hélène Bessette; *Le Dernier Homme* and *Thomas l'Obscur*, by Maurice Blanchot; *Les Vainqueurs du Jaloux*, by Jean Lagrolet; and *Le Maintien de l'ordre*, by Claude Ollier.

To Editions de Minuit for a passage from *La Mise en scène*, by Claude Ollier.

Translation of the selections from works unavailable in English is by the author. He has also translated the quotations from French periodicals.

# INTRODUCTION TO THE NEW NOVEL

*History of the Movement and Declaration of Its Aim*

The most significant development in recent French fiction is the "new novel," the *nouveau roman*, which was noticed first in the mid-1950's and has subsequently attained a notoriety important enough to consecrate it as an authentic avant-garde phenomenon. In 1961 it was placed on the program of the annual meeting of the Association Internationale des Etudes Françaises, and professors from all over the world came to hear Michel Butor, Bernard Pingaud, and foreign specialists discuss the new tendencies. The publication of *The Erasers* (1953), by Alain Robbe-Grillet, marks the beginning. This novel by a young scientist, new to literature, caught the critics' interest immediately. Although they detected echoes of Kafka, Simenon, and Graham Greene, they conceded that an extraordinary attention paid to objects, a total absence of moral preoccupation, and a curious treatment of time set the work distinctly apart. In newspaper interviews, the author accounted for the originality of his work on the grounds that it had been composed without the conventional device of "psychology" to present the characters and motivate the plot. *The Erasers* was a descriptive and scientific novel, Robbe-Grillet declared.

It soon became evident, although Robbe-Grillet maintained that he wrote first and theorized afterwards, that the originality of this novel rested on a quite specific and not unself-conscious esthetic and, moreover, that it implied definite philosophical convictions. Jean-Paul Sartre's sententious remark that a fictional technique is always based on the metaphysical attitude of the author is at least here patently applicable. Roland Barthes, who became Robbe-Grillet's chief spokesman, drew particular attention to the philosophical implications of *The Erasers* in a review article appearing in *Critique*, July, 1954. He pointed out that the objects described out of proportion to their normal significance in the novel are never allusive, never subjective, almost never used metaphorically. *The Erasers* is the novel of a man "who walks through the city with no horizon other than the spectacle, with no power other than that of his own eyes." In this universe dependent exclusively on a person's vision, time and space appear altered and interiority in all its expressions is abolished. Barthes concluded that, by its complete objectivity, this novel brings the art of French fiction up to the line of contemporary painting and the cinema.

Although Barthes continued to interpret Robbe-Grillet to the public, the author himself decided to explain his aims and views directly in a series of articles. He began by declaring that the surface of things must no longer be thought of as a mask for reality, but as the only reality we can grasp. The world is neither significant nor is it absurd—it just *is*. Objects are there, that is all, and it is improper to project ourselves into them, to personalize nature, as we have habitually done. The novelist today must limit himself to describing, measuring, defining objects as they appear to him. To this end he must forge a new technique and a new language. Such utterances could not fail to stir the critics, whom Robbe-Grillet had once declared in a state of lassitude before the traditional novel. But the feelings Robbe-Grillet inspired generally among the established reviewers or newspaper critics were those of hostility and indignation. André Rousseaux, Robert Kemp, and François Mauriac all treated his theories as pretentious and ridiculed his "laboratory" discussions.[1] Their indignation nevertheless served Robbe-Grillet's cause: public attention was thereby captured, and the new novel became the issue of the day. Critics favorable or unfavorable discussed the subject, identified Alain Robbe-Grillet as the leader of a new movement, placed under his banner a miscellany of writers chiefly

---

[1] See their columns in well-known French literary journals: Rousseaux and Mauriac in *Le Figaro Littéraire*, Kemp in *Les Nouvelles Littéraires*.

new and little known, and thereby created an avant-garde which would gather cohesion as it gathered momentum.

Bernard Dort, writing in 1955, associated with Robbe-Grillet the older, more established novelist Jean Cayrol and an unknown by the name of Paul Gadenne, and dubbed their works *romans blancs*. From the first inkling that a new movement was forming, critics began seeking an appropriate name and mulling over who belonged and who did not. Alain Bosquet picked up the word Sartre had coined to introduce *Portrait of a Man Unknown* by Nathalie Sarraute—*anti-roman*—and thought it described novels such as Maurice Blanchot's very well. Butor's novels, Pinget's, and Bessette's he would rather just call avant-garde. Gaëtan Picon disagreed with Sartre's application of the word anti-novel to Sarraute's book, but thought it fitted Michel Butor's *Passing Time* (*L'Emploi du Temps*). He preferred, however, the term *roman expérimental*. For Bernard Pingaud, the new novel was more *ante-roman* than *anti-roman*, since it constituted a sort of reflexion on what a novel should be. But, Pingaud declared, the writers in question have too little in common to justify Emile Henriot's referring to them as the "Ecole du regard." This invention of the veteran critic of *Le Monde* recalls Roland Barthes' *littérature objective*. Maurice Nadeau used the noncommittal term *jeune roman* and enlarged the group of "young" to include the playwright Samuel Beckett, the Algerian poet Kateb Yacine, and one Jacques Cousseau. A report published in the February, 1958, issue of *Arguments* avoided the problem of name by calling the subject of investigation merely "le roman d'aujourd'hui." Its articles deal mainly with Robbe-Grillet, Butor, and Sarraute, although Cayrol, Beckett, Claude Simon, and Marguerite Duras come into the picture. *Esprit's* more thorough report, published later the same year, used the title *nouveau roman* without hesitation or excuse and established a list of novelists who represent it. Ten was the number fixed: the seven just mentioned plus Yacine, Jean Lagrolet, and Robert Pinget.[2] But of course there can be

---

[2] One will find in the general bibliography (pp. 42–44) the texts on which this summary of the problem of a name and a membership is based.

nothing official or final about these choices. Claude Ollier should today be included, and every year new names can be added. The most recent to be mentioned in the French press are those of Marc Saporta, Jean Ricardou, and Daniel Castelain, fledgling authors who have identified themselves with the new writing. Others are brought into the movement by critics who quite rightly recognize the ever-spreading influence on all fiction writers. Thus Claude Mauriac is sometimes included, as well as Philippe Sollers, whose recent *Le Parc* has been cited as an example of "contamination."

The *Esprit* studies indicated how prodigiously important critical interest had become by 1958—so much so in fact that Gaëtan Picon felt called upon to protest against the "laborious exegesis covering today the fragile body of the new novel (an example of hyperbolic subtlety can be found in the special number of *Esprit*)." [3] As if in rebuke for this sort of mockery, Bernard Pingaud, on the editorial board of *Les Lettres Nouvelles*, declared that his magazine was warmly sympathetic to the new school and was ready to defend and foster *serious* criticism as opposed to the insouciant, subjective criticism of the newspaper variety. [4] Robbe-Grillet fanned the flame of public interest by lectures and radio discussions in which he was joined by Nathalie Sarraute, Michel Butor, and others. In 1958 and 1959, from the radio, the lecture platform, and in the press, the new novel was explained, discussed, and debated, with authors themselves taking a prominent part. [5] It is just as lively a subject today. In the *Revue de Paris* of September, 1961, Alain Robbe-Grillet addressed the general reader again, reviewing the aims and aspirations of his school in very direct and simple language and protesting against frequent misinterpretations on the part of the critics. The critics rose promptly to the bait.

The question which each critic has asked himself is what links all these new writers. Their frequent appearances together

---

[3] *Mercure de France*, December, 1958, p. 662.
[4] *Les Lettres Nouvelles*, April 8, 1959.
[5] For a typical discussion, see "Révolution dans le roman," *Le Figaro Littéraire*, March 29, 1958.

in public and before the microphone, the fact that many of them have a common publisher, the Editions de Minuit, suggest a united front. But these are external and incidental factors of unity—the real bond must be sought in their works. Noting the obvious differences they exhibit in their writing, some critics have hastily agreed with Robbe-Grillet that the new novelists are joined only in their voiced opposition to the conventional novel—that of the so-called Balzac tradition. There is unquestionably a link here in what they oppose. They all frown upon psychological analysis in the novel, social studies, story emphasis, devices for entertainment or escape. But there is also a link in what they admire. If these austere writers are united in a repudiation of the "traditional" novel, its aims and its methods, they are united also in a common enthusiasm for the untraditional novel as represented by Kafka, Joyce, Proust, and Faulkner, writers who have inspired some of their new techniques and preoccupations. Here, of course, is the significant bond: in spite of the individual differences which exist among the new writers, certain basic techniques and preoccupations are constant enough to be regarded as characteristic, and amply justify our thinking of them as a group. In broadest of terms, these techniques and preoccupations are those first detected in Robbe-Grillet's writing: a new approach to characters, disregard for chronology, prominence given to objects and space, substitution of pattern for plot, and unorthodox treatment of dialogue. Craftsmanship, in all its aspects, seems to be a matter of primary concern. But it is equally evident that new techniques are not just new ways to present old material; they are devices to express a new concept of the novel and a particular philosophical attitude.

The new novel aims first at destroying the old. This negative objective, implicit in any affirmation of a new esthetic concept, has received particular stress in discussions of the new novel both by the writers themselves and their critics. For Sartre, the new novel is the anti-novel; for Robbe-Grillet, its sole common denominator is its rejection of the conventional novel. Robbe-Grillet has perhaps led the attack with his thundering denunciations in the press, but Nathalie Sarraute is not far behind with her sarcastic article, "L'Ere du Soupçon." [6] They leave no doubt that they are bent on destruction and ultimately make themselves clear as to specifically what they would destroy. But the phrases bandied about by writers and critics alike tend to confuse by their vagueness and inexactitude. The target is described as the Balzacian novel, the traditional novel, the conventional novel, the psychological novel, quite indifferently, as if these terms all meant the same thing.

Consider first Robbe-Grillet's oft-quoted denunciation of Balzac and the "sacrosanct psychological tradition." This is a curious linking in view of Balzac's reputation for weakness in character portrayal. Countless other French novelists from Mme. de La Fayette to Proust might qualify better as psychological novelists. It is however not psychology as such the new writers object to—certainly not Mme. Sarraute at least—but rather to the literary technique of presenting characters from the outside, with the author standing between personage and reader to explain the former's thoughts to the latter. A term less general than psychology would be more appropriate to designate this technique they disapprove of, especially since a whole group of novels frequently called psychological in French manuals of literature do not characteristically use it. In *Obermann, Adolphe, Volupté*, etc., we find a confessional approach, with the first person singular utilized—precisely what the new novelists favor to avoid author intervention. To return to Balzac, we may wonder why he in particular is associated in Robbe-Grillet's mind with the convention of describing directly a character's thoughts. It was followed before him and has since been followed as a matter of course by writers who use the third person. Stendhal might have been a better choice than Balzac to symbolize the fictional technique under attack, for he is a writer famous for his "psychology" and,

[6] First published in *Les Temps Modernes*, February, 1950, it appeared in a volume of essays with the over-all title *L'Ere du Soupçon* (Gallimard, 1956).

moreover, one who habitually uses the analytic summary to present his characters' thoughts and sentiments. Finally, we may note, it is confusing and paradoxical, particularly for Anglo-American readers, that the French avant-garde attack be aimed nominally at psychology, although consciousness is unquestionably the subject of their own works. When an American professor writes a book about the English-language novelists who precede the new French school in taking consciousness as their domain (James, Woolf, Dorothy Richardson, Joyce, Faulkner), he calls it *The Psychological Novel.*[7]

Perhaps "realistic novel" would more exactly describe what the new novelists oppose, since they do not approve of objective presentation of character or setting. This term would do, were it not that they are equally disapproving of story and fictional invention, features of entertainment already minimized by the great nineteenth-century French realists and naturalists. "Traditional novel," which is a term sometimes used to designate the object of attack, might also seem satisfactory at first glance. But what tradition is meant? Novels after Mme. de La Fayette? after Dumas? after Balzac? after Zola? There is obviously no one sort of traditional novel. "Conventional novel" is probably the best word for their specific target, for what the new novelists seem really to have in mind is the popular novel of entertainment such as it has developed during the course of the twentieth century, a novel which combines techniques from the realistic tradition and from the analytical tradition to present what this new generation of novelists denounce as a superficial and false picture of life. But in their eagerness to proclaim the need for something new, there is nothing from the past that will really do. This accounts, I should say, for their vagueness and the impropriety of their terms. This accounts, moreover, for their utterly false representation of the twentieth-century French novel.

In listening to Robbe-Grillet, one would think that the only fiction in recent French history had been the best seller, that the French novel had not evolved since Paul Bourget. Yet the

[7] Leon Edel. Lippincott, 1955.

novel represented by Robbe-Grillet as overdue for liquidation had been liquidated for many years. Neither *The Counterfeiters*, *Man's Fate* (*La Condition humaine*), *Siegfried and the Limousin*, nor *The Wanderer* (*Le Grand Meaulnes*) fits the description; and Valéry's famous remark that he had written no novels because he could not bring himself to write, "The Marquise went out at five o'clock," may have been uttered before Robbe-Grillet was born. The significant French novelists had already begun to reject the formulas of the romanticists and the realists very early in the century; in the period between the wars, writers, sensitive to new conceptions of reality and of personality, oriented the novel away from Balzac, Stendhal, and their more recent successors, Anatole France and Paul Bourget. Robbe-Grillet urged a violent rupture with the past; as a matter of fact the French novel had been evolving towards the new novel for many years.

To be sure we may expect new writers to overstate their case and exaggerate the originality of their program. It is the usual thing to see each generation set forth to slay the monster we thought already slain. But if it seems surprising that Robbe-Grillet and the others often speak as if the great French authors of the twentieth century were merely imitators of Honoré de Balzac, it seems even more so that they ignore almost completely in their discussions those writers across the Channel like James, Richardson, and Woolf, whom they should hail as spiritual parents. Henry James and Joseph Conrad had destroyed, for English literature, the simple story directly told and, in presenting the mental life of their personages, had invented techniques that anticipate the new French novel. James's "rendering" rather than reporting, his concern with the uniform point of view, Conrad's placing the narrator inside the story to interpret and refract it were steps along the way. Although Mme. Sarraute considers Virginia Woolf very much dated, she must grant that the author of *To the Lighthouse* and *Mrs. Dalloway* was a pioneer in repudiating the "psychology" Mme. Sarraute holds in horror. In England the "era of suspicion" began some time ago and, like Nathalie Sarraute herself, Virginia Woolf was aware of the strange associational workings of the mind and the instability of the ego. Richardson's stream-of-consciousness technique also took the novel far away from Victorian conventions. There were others besides Faulkner and Joyce in the English "impressionistic" advance-guard: the new French writers owe their elders at least a bow. One might wonder whether they do not believe that it was Jean-Paul Sartre who first objected to the author acting omniscient in his novel, that Sartre had found a unique example when he showed how Faulkner in *The Sound and the Fury* works through the mind of his characters.

Compared to Robbe-Grillet and Nathalie Sarraute, Michel Butor has attacked less and explained more fully what his aims in writing amount to. A novel for Butor is an instrument of knowledge, he tells us, particularly in his article, "Le roman comme recherche." [8] No longer a pastime or luxury, a novel is primarily a means of comprehending experience. In another article, "L'Ecriture pour moi est une colonne vertébrale," [9] Butor explains how he uses the novel as a means of exploring his problems through concrete examples. He writes in the hope of elucidating his problems, of organizing and supporting his existence. As Roquentin had said in Sartre's *Nausea:* "Keep a diary to see clearly." [10]

Claude Simon, too, since the success of *The Flanders Road*, has expounded his concept of the novel in interviews and addresses. He tries, with great patience, to fit the pieces he possesses into a pattern, to reconstruct a person's story and his soul from bits of hearsay and chance encounters. It is clear that, for all the new novelists, writing is primarily a means of seeking reality and their own situation in the world. Nathalie Sarraute peers beneath the commonplaces of social conversation (Heidegger's "babble," as Sartre called it) to come closer to the "authentic" personality. Maurice Blanchot studies language with the same in mind. Robbe-Grillet's world of objects is only the world as it

[8] *Cahiers du Sud*, 1955, pp. 349–354. Reprinted in *Répertoire* (Editions de Minuit, 1960).
[9] *Les Nouvelles Littéraires*, February 5, 1959.
[10] New Directions, 1949, p. 7.

appears refracted through the consciousness of his protagonists: his purpose does not differ from Roquentin's, whose vision at times is already pure "Robbe-Grillet": ". . . here is a cardboard box holding my bottle of ink. I should try to tell how I saw it *before* and now how I . . . Well, it's a parallelepiped rectangle." [11] Claude Ollier's aim in writing is manifestly the same as that of Robbe-Grillet and the others.

This metaphysical ambition, so clearly implied by what the new novelists say and do, has characterized the French novel for several decades. In Germaine Bree's book on the modern novel,[12] we can read that, from Cocteau and Malraux forth, writers have used the novel as a means of organizing a frail existence constantly threatened by disintegration and nothingness. The new philosopher-novelists mark the most recent and extreme point in this development to make the novel serve philosophical ends. We say extreme point because the new writers are free from the political, ethical, or sociological involvements that caught up their predecessors. Critics like Bernard Dort exaggerate when they stress the political implications of the new novel.[13] Condemning the "conventional" novel is only very indirectly condemning the bourgeoisie. No matter how antibourgeois the new writers might be in personal sentiment, their works never carry a patent social message, and it would be improper to view Marguerite Duras' *The Sea Wall* (*Un Barrage contre le Pacifique*) as a diatribe against colonialism or Sarraute's *Tropismes* as social satire. All the new novelists would doubtless agree with Claude Simon when he says, "The novelist that I am is absolutely foreign to politics." [14] Robbe-Grillet does not hesitate to speak for others as well as for himself: "It is not reasonable . . . to claim to serve a political cause in our novels, even a cause that seems to us

[11] *Nausea*, p. 7
[12] Germaine Brée and Margaret Guiton, *An Age of Fiction* (Rutgers University Press, 1957).
[13] See his article in *Les Lettres Françaises* of May 8, 1958, translated by Kenneth Douglas for *Yale French Studies*, 24. For an interesting discussion of the new novel as a sociological phenomenon—a different matter—see Jean Bloch-Michel, "Nouveau roman et culture des masses," *Preuves*, March, 1961, pp. 17–28. Also Pierre-Henri Simon, "Sur le sens de l'antiroman," *Preuves*, May, 1961, pp. 52–55.
[14] Bourin, André. "Techniciens du roman: Claude Simon," *Les Nouvelles Littéraires*, December 29, 1960.

a just one, even if in our political life we fight for its triumph." [15] The cogitations of their elders brought them soon to preaching— Christian virtue, moral liberty, action, and, most recently, participation or engagement. Today's writers do not give solutions or recommendations, but keep their gaze fixed on the inner life with all the single-mindedness of the pure scientist.

Although they ignore completely the "engagement" preached by Jean-Paul Sartre, they appear in all else to be his most faithful disciples. Most of them, whether they recognize their debt or not, are of an age to remember that *Nausea* was one of the great experiences of their youth and that Sartre's essays on philosophy and literary criticism set their own standards of value. It was Sartre who in the first place said that things *are* before they are something, who denounced authors who play God in a well-ordered universe (Mauriac) and authors who believe in a well-ordered universe (Giraudoux). Sartre's concept of personality and his outlook on the world proliferate throughout the works of the new novelists. And it was he who suggested to them that a novel could be a vehicle for pure philosophical investigation and that faithful, unbiased description is the method to follow. Accordingly, no prejudices, no preconceived notions, no assumptions are permitted to color the data that the new novelists record of their experience. Their goal is to describe only— objectively, scientifically, as completely as possible. They vow, like Roquentin, not to let a thing escape: "Nuances or small happenings . . . even though they might seem to mean nothing." [16] When an author finishes his book, he has given us a glimpse of how reality appeared to him at a given moment and of how he tried to make some sense of it.

If the new writers state their repudiations and aspirations overdramatically and ignore their place in literary history as a product of a long and slow evolution, this does not make their works any less interesting or important. This does not, moreover, make their works any less original. The French novel was

---

[15] "Le Nouveau roman," *La Revue de Paris*, September, 1961, p. 121.
[16] *Nausea*, p. 7

oriented towards the metaphysical before the new novel; the English novel had already made use of stream-of-consciousness techniques. But developing these techniques in the service of philosophy is indeed something new. It has led to profound modifications in all aspects of the novel.

*Human Nature, Psychology, and the Art of Characterization*

The abandonment of the "classic notion of man" has been widely recognized as a feature of the new novel. Sometimes this appears to mean the abandonment of the notion of human nature as an absolute or as a norm, as an essence independent of, or prior to, man's existence—the concept Sartre attacks on metaphysical grounds. René Marill Albérès may have this in mind when he states that the new novelists' refusal of psychology is a refusal of the humanistic centuries. Camille Bourniquel, in presenting the new novel in *Esprit*,[17] obviously holds this interpretation: "It is a certain notion of man, the intelligibility of the created world, which are this time in the balance. How can we remain strangers to this degradation of the person, to this 're-jection of human nature'!" The humanistic ideal is surely absent from the new novels. We could not say today what Walter Besant prissily said in England in the eighties: "It is, fortunately, not possible in this country for any man to defile and defame humanity and still be called an artist."[18] But then neither could we have said it at that time in France, which is the time of Zola. We must not exaggerate the esteem human nature may be presumed to have enjoyed in the past. Neither the Christian Middle Ages nor modern times when the theories of sensationalism and determinism prevailed can be said to have consistently contributed to its exaltation. Yet there is a difference; for, if medieval man was a miserable sinner, he had nevertheless been created in the image of God, and even the creature of the "scientists" was the product of

[17] "Le 'nouveau roman,'" *Esprit*, July–August, 1958, p. 2.
[18] See Walter Besant and Henry James, *The Art of Fiction* (Boston: De Wolfe, Fiske & Co., 1884), p. 29.

plans and laws. Nothing, however, is behind the wretch of today, as he is depicted in the new novel.

By abandoning the "classic notion of man," however, what seems more often meant is the abandonment of the notion of an integral and fixed personality. Of course protest against this notion is centuries old. Buddhist thinkers had rejected the idea that the self could be a substance; in western culture it has frequently been questioned since Hume and the *Treatise on Human Nature*. In the twentieth century the recrudescence of personalism and the rise of psychoanalysis have made it quite untenable. Stream-of-consciousness authors, Marcel Proust and many others, all demonstrate as much. Even in François Mauriac's heroes, to mention the writer Sartre specifically attacked for treating his characters as absolutes, there are elements of ambiguity and ambivalence which keep them from being precise or static. Yet, despite the evidence to the contrary, the notion of self as a hard, indissoluble unit stubbornly persists in the popular mind, and the new generation of writers takes up the cudgels again.

The characteristic technique of French novelists has been, they insist, to study personality in depth, cutting through the outer layers in order to bring to light its true nature. The results have never been successful, for the simple reason that there is no true nature to discover. We might object here incidentally that the classic ambition of fiction was really more modest, amounting to no more than showing contrasts between what people seem viewed from the social angle and what they really are "underneath." In exposing hypocrisy, etc., novelists doubtless fully succeeded in doing what they aimed to do; it may be questioned whether the stereotyped imagery of surface and depth really implied as much as the new novelists would see in it. We have a similar question when we hear new novelists score the practice of presenting characters as types, suspecting that the matter is one more of esthetic expediency than psychological intent. Here we become involved in justifications of simplification, stylization, etc., for artistic reasons. But, in principle at least, we shall have to admit that presenting types and well-defined characters does assume the notion of integral personality; on this basis the new novelists condemn the technique as falsifying and oversimplifying life.

"Characters," Madame Sarraute declares, "such as the old novel conceived them (and all the old apparatus used to show them off) no longer succeed in containing psychological reality." [19] There is no good person, no bad person, no miser, but each one is all at one and the same time. Instead of a hard kernel of personality, the new authors find an ever-changing, ever-fluid stream of sentiments and instincts common to all humanity. Jean Cayrol says, "No one would think today of painting the miser, the jealous man, or the timid man: we are all that at once. What we can try to do is catch an individual at a particular psychological instant." [20] The psychological element or phenomenon has replaced the individual as the unit to be studied. "So, by an evolution like that of painting—although infinitely more timid and slow, marked by long pauses and backsliding—the psychological element, like the pictorial element, is insensibly freeing itself from the object to which it used to belong. It is tending to be sufficient unto itself and to get along as much as possible without support. On it the novelist concentrates all his search, on it the reader must concentrate all his attention." [21]

To root out the false notion of personality, the new novelists eschew all the devices used by other novelists to set the personage before your eyes. No vital statistics, no photographic descriptions, a minimum of individualization. In *L'Ere du Soupçon*, Nathalie Sarraute comments on the increasing anonymity of the characters in a novel. Gide avoided patronyms, Kafka and Joyce used initials, Faulkner gave two characters the same name. Now in the new novels, the "I" is quite imprecise and the secondary characters are without autonomous existence. Sarraute's own characters possess no individual frontiers, and until *The Planetarium*, the reader could never be sure who was talking in

[19] *L'Ere du Soupçon*, p. 71.
[20] Interviewed by André Bourin in *Les Nouvelles Littéraires*, May 21, 1959.
[21] *L'Ere du Soupçon*, p. 71.

her novels. All the traditional means of defining the character in the everyday world are avoided if they are not, as in the case of dialogue, used merely to show that the social, individualized man is a fake, a network "of conventional opinions, received as is from the group to which he belongs." [22] What passes as individual configuration of personality appears to the new novelists as superficial as age, occupation, or place of dwelling—surface matters either to be ignored or lumped together to constitute the "inauthentic" person which they are eager to expose. This explains Sartre's "bastards" and the babblers of Sarraute and Duras, whose platitudes in social conversation cover a squirming mass of sentiments and feelings nameless and common to all. The reader must never be permitted the illusion that he is seeing a character as an individual or that he has a complete view of his personality.

It is because of their conviction that personality cannot be defined or so encompassed that the new writers have objected violently to the "analytical" technique. The point-of-view technique seems to them more honest and more true to life. Interior monologue, conversation, or stream-of-consciousness replace the long expository paragraphs in which the writer, standing aloof from his characters and knowing all about them, explains what they are really like. The writer and the reader are now inside the story, not outside, and inside the character, so as never to get a complete look at him. We slide into the skin of the young Frenchman in *Passing Time* and see the English city of Bleston through his eyes; we become the salesman in *The Voyeur*, and if we miss the point of the story until it is over, it is because we have to wait until then to regain the use of our own eyes. If we do not know that the hero of Lagrolet's *Les Vainqueurs du Jaloux* is an unlovely person, it is because he himself is under the illusion that he is rather noble.

In equating psychology with exposition or direct analysis, the new novelists have, to be sure, created confusion and bewilderment. No matter how they conceive of it, the human mind is still the subject of their own fiction—hence psychology. It

[22] *L'Ere du Soupçon*, p. 12.

might have been better had they said that their quarrel was with analytical psychology; then we could properly call the new writing descriptive psychology to differentiate between the two. Metapsychology might also be a good word for the new writing, since it studies psychology at the level where psychology mingles with epistemology. And yet when we consider how strongly the word psychology today connotes scientific assumptions and methodology—hypothesis, demonstration, conclusion, etc.—and how foreign all this is to the new novel, we must decide that the word psychology in any form is not the right one. The new novel, limiting itself to recording the reactions of a consciousness without any conceptual assumptions whatever follows so exactly the philosophical method advocated by Edmund Husserl and popularized in France by Sartre that the word phenomenology seems the only one which will do. The complex question of psychology and the new novel resolves itself in this—psychology has been replaced by phenomenology.

The new novelists' rejection of the analytical method of presenting characters is postulated upon the same philosophic rejection of ideality that motivated Edmund Husserl in the first years of this century to reject neo-Kantism. Husserl, before Sartre or any of the new writers, had said that the world is there before it is anything. But the world to be there is not to be fully autonomous. The world is there only because it is perceived by human consciousness, which gives it its significance and its reality. Inversely, consciousness is nothing without the world, since consciousness means consciousness of something. In treating the world as existing outside consciousness and putting consciousness into the world, so to speak, not as a thing but as a sort of illumination of things, Husserl opposes the idealistic and rationalistic concept of the inner man, abstract and immutable. Merleau-Ponty, the French phenomenologist, declares, "Truth does not 'reside' only in the 'inner man,' or rather there is no inner man, man is in the world, it is in the world that he knows himself. When I come back to myself from the dogmatism of common sense or from the dogmatism of science, I find not a focal center of intrinsic truth, but a subject committed to the world." [23] In his essay, "A Fundamental Idea of Husserl," Sartre proclaimed that Husserl's notion of the "intentional" consciousness had delivered us from interiority. What this means to the new novelists is the destruction of a fixed and given human nature, a personality as such, and the fragmentation of consciousness in the world. For a Robbe-Grillet, who repeats Sartre's exultant cry that interiority is abolished and that things *are* before they are something, there seems nothing left but the human eye roving over the world.

Robbe-Grillet demonstrates perhaps more obviously than the others the repudiation of the subjective, essentialist point of reference. Not only has he filled his novels with minute descriptions of objects devoid of intrinsic human values and qualities, but, in his essays, by damning and derisive phrases like "suspect interiority" and "the romantic heart of things" (borrowed from Barthes), he has struck repeatedly at subjectivism. All the new novelists, however, follow the method and the objective that Husserl formulated when he proposed returning to things. The method is completely neutral, postulating no realistic or idealistic metaphysic—nothing, as Robbe-Grillet says, that would imply essentialism or pre-established order. It amounts merely to a description of the world such as it appears to a completely naïve consciousness. The writer's purpose is the same as the philosopher's: to depict the world as it is illuminated by consciousness and to depict consciousness itself in its act of perceiving and giving sense to the world. One may well ask oneself here if the new writers are not in fundamental error esthetically and perhaps psychologically in equating their task with that of existential philosophers. Exclusive use of what the narrator feels and sees denies the reader basic information that the narrator himself already possesses. The hero of Claude Ollier's *Le Maintien de l'ordre*, for example, knows who he is, why he is being pursued, etc. Why make the reader guess? We are more than recording consciousnesses to ourselves and, if we are really to identify ourselves with the hero, we should be more properly "cued in."

[23] See Gaëtan Picon, *Panorama des idées contemporaines* (Gallimard, 1957), p. 66.

But properly or not, the traditional hero of the novel has become just a recording consciousness. His identity is purposely imprecise, since, as a subject of philosophical demonstration, he must represent consciousness as such rather than any particular one defined by age, sex, or situation. This anonymity, we might note incidentally, is what differentiates him from the stream-of-consciousness hero of Woolf or even of Joyce. With these authors, as with Henry James, it is a particular mind that is being exposed and a particular pair of eyes that is viewing the world. The new novelists, attempting rather to portray everybody's mind, have to stay with basic situations and general sentiments and, if they are to avoid the sort of objection made above concerning *Le Maintien de l'ordre*, select for their hero a type which will portray experience as directly, as naïvely, as possible. Now since one sort of person is more plausibly reduced to a recording consciousness than another, there has evolved in the new novel a type hero whom readers are most likely to accept as spokesman for humanity.

Typically the new hero is an outsider whose processes differ from those of the social animal moved by group awarenesses and reflexes. Roquentin, of Sartre's *Nausea*, and Meursault, of Camus' *The Outsider*,[24] can be regarded as prototypes, both solitary men whose isolation makes them ideally serve their purpose. Devoid of obligations in the world, of ambitions, illusions, or codes of abstract values, they can ideally offer a mirror of consciousness at work. Roquentin, the celibate scholar, incarnates the active intelligence, observing, noting, and judging. In his quest for reality, his search for meaning in what he observes and feels, he anticipates Butor's heroes in *Passing Time* and *A Change of Heart* and Robbe-Grillet's detective in *The Erasers*. He stands behind Robert Pinget's hero in *Monsieur Levert*, too, and Lagrolet's young architect in *Les Vainqueurs du Jaloux*. Meursault, the obscure office worker, is (until his moment of revolt) a passive

[24] Translated as *The Stranger* in the American edition (Alfred A. Knopf, 1946).

intelligence, typifying the purest and most naïve of responses. Jean Cayrol's Armand and Claude Simon's Antoine Montès are of the same sort. But whether he descends from Roquentin or from Meursault, the new hero veers towards the type of solitary, unattached person, who will not or cannot remain with the herd.

When one thinks, by way of comparison, of the heroes of the old romances, paragons of perfections, it seems ridiculous to use the same word for these social misfits, particularly among the progeny of Meursault. Armand, Jean Cayrol's hero, is a brutish vagrant, and he has many companions in the novel of to-day. Pierre de Boisdeffre thus characterizes the new antihero: "In the novel of today, the bum has taken the place of the hero. Misfits and the underprivileged have replaced the rich gallery of characters that goes from Julien Sorel to the heroes of Tolstoy: exemplary or not, the hero of fiction was called, if not to holiness, to love, or to genius, at least to taste the riches of the world, the pleasures of action and the joys of thought, to live in fellowship with other men, to share their sufferings and their hopes. The hero of *On Vous Parle* has become the symbol of a fallen humankind, that eats furtively, sleeps furtively, endures life and does not dominate it—a man to whom nothing beckons, who does not know how to laugh, who dares not love, who has known of existence only its seamy side, its humiliations. . . . From the likable and pitiable hero of Jean Cayrol to the atrocious bums of Samuel Beckett, the road is thronged where distress gets only worse." [25]

Perhaps Kafka's heroes should be mentioned as prototypes as well as those of Sartre and Camus, for the anxiety they suffer is shared by many heroes of today's novels, whose wretchedness is rendered more acute by apprehensiveness and feelings of guilt. Not knowing whence they come, what they are going to, Armand and his brothers in Beckett, Robbe-Grillet, and the others are racked by fear. To demonstrate the philosophical apprehensiveness that Sartre describes as inherent to the condition of mankind, the new novelists have found the most plausible subjects in

[25] *Une Histoire vivante de la littérature d'aujourd'hui* (Le Livre Contemporain, 1958), p. 368.

the foreigner, the pariah, and the unfit. The hero-consciousness of *Martereau* and *Portrait of a Man Unknown* is among the last named, a weakling trembling and cowering in his room, prey to all the monsters of his imagination. His neurotic sensibility tells him that all the world judges him a misfit, a sorry excuse for a man. Human abasement reaches its lowest level in Beckett's heroes, so immobile and helpless that one wonders whether they are not already dead and whether their whimperings are not the wails of ghosts.

Such is the hero-type in the new novel. Demanding first of all a recording consciousness, writers have found in the anonymous outsider a perfect subject. He may simply be a foreigner, such as Butor's young Frenchman in Bleston, but most characteristically his isolation involves degradation of some sort, for he must represent as generally and authentically as possible what today's philosophers regard as the human condition. Robbe-Grillet and Claude Simon have, in their recent novels, both chosen to depict a soldier separated from his company after rout and defeat, a dazed creature bereft of dignity by hunger and exhaustion, grotesque in ragbag garments of miscellaneous provenance. If no one can speak any longer of personality and human nature, one can still speak of the human condition, the universality of which is vouched for by Jean-Paul Sartre. And this is everywhere defined in the new fiction as wretchedness and farcicality. *Homo absurdus*, says Nathalie Sarraute, like old Karamazov acting the fool in Father Zossima's cell, now standing proudly, then twisting, hopping, gesticulating and grimacing, never sure whether he is serious or play-acting.

Apart from the recording consciousness which is the central personage, there are no characters of consequence in the typical new novel. Other persons come into view only when the hero is looking at them, their existence entirely dependent upon his consciousness. Some may excite our curiosity in a tantalizing fashion, like Rose, in Claude Simon's novel, *The Wind*, but we are never allowed to look at her directly. The new writers are not interested in furthering our social acquaintances and disapprove, on principle, of the conventional secondary and peripheral characters going about when the narrator's eye is not upon them.

Mme. Sarraute refers ironically to the versatility novelists have assumed for themselves in creating independent secondary characters. Readers are well aware, she declares in *L'Ere du Soupçon*, that novelists have just parceled out bits of themselves to do so, and concludes that it would be more honest to forego this multiple disguise. Flaubert could well say, "Bovary c'est moi," because an author, at bottom, knows only himself. The question she raises is a complex one and involves main characters as well as secondary ones: to what degree can or should a writer invent another personality? On the one hand, it goes without saying that no writer can get completely out of himself; on the other, he cannot of course be limited to autobiography. The question is, moreover, as pertinent to stream-of-consciousness novels as to any other sort, since in them the part of invention can be just as great. We would not identify a sadist killer or a jealous husband with Robbe-Grillet; a middle-aged businessman planning to leave his wife, with Michel Butor; even Nathalie Sarraute's personages with herself. And the presumption of being able to enter another mind is surely as great as that of describing a person and analyzing him externally. Even if the reader does "suspend disbelief" for one character, he may be far more "suspicious" of a miscellany of characters whose inner life he is invited to behold than of incidental characters set in everyday reality. A Balzac can describe and conjecture about any number of persons without offending credibility, but the stream-of-consciousness technique imposes much stricter limitations. When Virginia Woolf darts about from one mind to another, with the idea of focusing different views on a given topic, we know she is inventing.

The French novelists of the new school sometimes move, too, from one character to another, but not for the purpose of emphasizing differences between individuals. The moves may be so unobtrusive that the reader is not even aware of them. Often, I have said, he is not even sure who is thinking or talking. It is questionable whether the French technique is more convincing.

Mme. Sarraute maintains that the new novelists work at a depth that dissolves all differences between individuals, but this can only be true as far as basic urges, drives, etc., are concerned. Not differentiating one person's thoughts from another's and parcelling out consciousness among several may seem to the reader a practice as dishonest as any. In *Passage de Milan,* where Butor weaves in and out of the minds of a dozen people, it is disturbing to find their monologues all in the same brutally realistic and cynical tone, which is surely not appropriate to all the dwellers in that apartment house or to humanity as such. It is fortunate that most often the new novelists, like Butor in the two novels that followed *Passage de Milan,* stay with one consciousness and keep the other characters flat.

*Structure and Narrative Device*

No matter what the writer's aim may be or the aspect of life he treats, the heart of fiction remains the story—that is to say, what the characters do and what happens to them. Physical in *The Three Musketeers,* psychological in *Princess of Cleves,* sociological in *Germinal,* the novel remains an adventure of one sort or another. The new novel, dedicated to epistemological ends, records *a* metaphysical adventure if not *the* metaphysical adventure.

Needless to say, the intention and disposition of the writer—psychological, sociological, or whatever—commit the adventure to certain proportions and to a certain configuration. The Dumas type of story progresses by means of the multiple episode; the La Fayette, by the unfolding of character and the situations that character creates; the Zola, by demonstration of cause and effect in the world of social phenomena. Inherent in each type are its requirements for length and breadth, a suitable beginning, time span, and ending. The new novel has, like the others, evolved a characteristic narrative form to meet the requirements posed by new aims and preoccupations.

In a work like *Je vivrai l'amour des autres,* it is obvious that behind Armand's adventure, Jean Cayrol is narrating the great epic of all mankind, his slow emergence from an incogitant state. Beginning with physical sensations, this pre-Adamic hero becomes gradually aware of objects and living things. We read on the fly-leaf of the third volume, *Le Feu qui prend:* "Whereas in the first two volumes . . . Armand was evolving in a universe of objects hostilely or kindly disposed, now he is suddenly awake to all that makes man, destroys him, or glorifies him. Beasts raise surprised eyes on this 'humiliated child'; beings greet him, a woman offers him the chance to live his own love. . . . Armand is here only a man among us, . . . for there is no broken space between beings." The man's evolvement can be measured by his manner of loving. Long in the infantile stage where the ego and the non-ego are not clearly defined, he loved anonymously and parasitically (hence the title), but now, with sharpened awarenesses, he can know the torments of jealousy and will tolerate no one between Lucette and himself. Samuel Beckett's nondramatic pieces move in an opposite direction, depict not man's ascent but his descent, and show him returning to a level of consciousness even lower than where, in Jean Cayrol, he started. The story Beckett tells over and over in *Molloy, Malone,* etc., is the final disintegration and collapse of the rational faculties. Novels by other new writers are less epic in scope, but they all mirror or interpret aspects of the human adventure, man's search to know and understand. Such is the story of *Passing Time,* in which Jacques Revel struggles to get at reality behind all the clues that confuse him, the signs that he encounters as he walks the streets of the English cathedral town. It is the story, too, of *The Erasers,* in which Wallas tries desperately to solve the puzzle of the port city as he walks along its streets.

These meanderings—long walks through lonely streets— are favorite patterns to depict man's sojourn on earth. French writers here seem to be in James Joyce's debt; for, like Bloom, from Roquentin to the soldier in *In the Labyrinth,* the heroes of the new novel are mainly deambulatory. The impetus may be without precision—Cayrol's heroes seem to wander aimlessly, simply viewing. Others, although they remain chiefly registering consciousnesses, are in pursuit of something—a Gibraltar sailor (Marguerite Duras' novel) or a Nedjma (Kateb Yacine). Others are after the solution to some mystery, and here the odyssey pattern combines with that of the detective story to establish the plot. *The Erasers, Passing Time, La Mise en Scène* owe something to Conan Doyle and his successors. In this last novel, by Claude Ollier, the author-engineer, who is surveying for a road across the African desert, tries to reconstruct the circumstances of his predecessor's mysterious death and the stabbing of a native girl. But, differing from the detective story, these novels fail to establish with certainty that there has been any murder, and the eerie atmosphere through which the engineer, like Jacques Revel and Wallas, blindly gropes after the truth is more suggestive of the hallucinatory universe of Franz Kafka's works than of the prosy, everyday world which serves as background for most modern crime and mystery novels.

Unlike the detective story, moreover, these novels of quest are not contrived fictions intended to keep the reader from guessing the ending as long as possible. For the new novelist does not himself know what the ending is going to be. He must invent as he proceeds; for, if his characters are to be true according to his philosophy, he must hold no preconceived notion of what is going to happen to them. Butor defined the novel as a search, and Sartre said the only true novel was of duration. Both specifications are admirably met by the quest structure, but to advance otherwise than by improvisation would falsify the human adventure, which the new novel aims to depict, and fail to demonstrate the "everlasting becoming" character of man stressed by existentialism. If we look closely at one of Cayrol's novels—say, *La Noire*—we see how fortuitously the episodes develop. Within the limits of beginning and ending, which Cayrol arbitrarily sets for his novels, the heroine's adventures are invented as the story progresses. Simon's Faulknerian tales likewise give a strong impression of being invented as they go along. Marguerite Duras says about her own novels, "I advance only with uncertainty." [26] Ionesco could be speaking for the novelists when he says of himself, "For me any play is an adventure, a hunt, the discovery of a universe that reveals itself to me, at the presence of which I am the first to be astounded." [27] It is as if, once created by their author, the characters in the new French novel are left to shift for themselves, as free to manage their destiny as Sartre declares human beings to be.

Marguerite Duras speaks of her quest novels as novels of a miracle expected but not accomplished. It is true that in *La Vie tranquille* the hopes for making the farm prosper dwindle away, in *Un Barrage contre le Pacifique* (*The Sea Wall*) the ocean is not held back, in *Les petits chevaux de Tarquinia* the vacationers never make the trip to view the frieze. Differing again from the detective story, the search upon which the new novel is structured ends in failure. Neither Butor's Jacques Revel, his Pierre Eller, nor Lagrolet's Gilles ever succeeds in unifying his experience of the world. The father in Pinget's novel never gets the letter written to his son, any more than Sartre's historian succeeds in writing his book. We are left in the dark as to the fate of Robbe-Grillet's heroes, not knowing whether the murderer is punished in *The Voyeur* or whether the situation in *Jealousy* is eventually resolved. The mysterious parcel which the soldier in *In the Labyrinth* carries contains nothing of interest, and the novel just peters out. Novelists of events traditionally closed their book when the events were over, and novelists of psychological crisis stopped when the crisis was over. The sociological novelists borrowed their endings from the other two. But the new French writers, eschewing the sort of resolution inherent in plot, must rely, like the English stream-of-consciousness novelists before them, upon purely arbitrary devices. *The Erasers* takes place within twenty-four hours and *Passing Time*, one full year. *A Change of Heart* is over when the train pulls into the station. At the expiration moment, these books are finished. Presumably they could have gone on

[26] See André Bourin, "Les Enfants du demi-siècle," *Les Nouvelles Littéraires,* June 18, 1959.
[27] *Impromptu de l'Alma* (Théâtre II, Gallimard, 1958), p. 13

indefinitely, but without tying the threads together or ever offering a conventional ending.

If external time—clock time—serves to establish the boundaries of a new novel, it is subjective time—duration—which operates within the novel and constitutes a factor in its internal structure. The mind lengthens or shortens episode, jumbles past, present, and future, and since the business of this novel is to record consciousness, its inner course resembles that of the mindstream. This accounts for the repetition of scenes in works such as *The Voyeur* and *Jealousy*—the author reintroduces the scene each time it recurs in the narrator's consciousness—and for the anachronistic sequence of scenes noticeable everywhere in the new fiction. As the mind registers what the eye sees, the memory comes into play, and perhaps the imagination as well. This simultaneous activity is set down as such; for, as Claude Simon insisted in an interview,[28] the integral experience must be preserved.

The rejection of chronology in favor of the ways of consciousness has, of course, its reason in philosophy. The subject of time has been one of phenomenology's favorite themes. Heidegger made time as it is experienced by the individual the basic category of existence. Human life, he argued, is lived under the shadow of time, for man alone among living creatures anticipates his death and is aware of the constant alterations he undergoes both physically and mentally during the course of his existence. Sartre saw the novel, always a tract of time, as the means of showing man as the time-haunted creature that philosophy conceived him to be. Declaring that the only true novel is one of duration, he placed the novel squarely in the service of philosophy and established the foundation for the narrative progression the new novelists favor. Butor and Simon are most clearly philosophers of time. Their books translate very exactly what is called the phenomenological "reflexion," that is, the attempt to reconstruct an experience retained by memory and to arrive at its significance by describing it as fully as possible. But Robbe-Grillet, too, by repeating scenes, follows the phenomenological teaching that by

[28] Madeleine Chapsal, "Entretien avec Claude Simon," *Express*, November 10, 1960.

invoking the phenomenon repeatedly one may summon its meaning. Other novelists, while less obviously demonstrating philosophical lessons, nevertheless are guided in their narrative by subjective time rather than by chronology.

In defining an arrangement of scene and episode which ignores rational categories, we are apt to liken it to that of dreams, for it is in dreams that we can see most clearly the processes of the mind operate without intellectual bias or interference. On the grounds of its oneiric quality, we might call the new novel the surrealistic novel par excellence. Our impression of experiencing a dream as we read is intensified by the sustained point of view, a narrative device which the new novelists consider basic in their art. We remain walled up in the narrator's consciousness, never permitted to consult with the author or to depart even momentarily to get an outsider's look at the situation. No one tells us what actually happened or is going to happen. The hero is never sure whether a certain speech was actually spoken, whether his sense lied or his interpretation was erroneous. All he can do, from his limited point of view, is to conjecture. "Perhaps," "probably," "doubtless" stud his sentences to show the reader he does not know the truth himself. As we follow his unsure steps, we feel we are losing our foothold in the real, that we are in a dream or that we are victims of hallucination. The world that the hero constructs laboriously out of personal experience or hearsay can only be tentative, and we fear it may crumble before our eyes like those illusory worlds of Japanese legend. *In the Labyrinth,* for instance, reads like the nightmare of the ill and dying soldier.

Here again we find Sartre and philosophy behind a technique. "In the real novel . . . there is no place for a privileged observer," he had declared,[29] taking his stand on the grounds that since absolute truth cannot be known, the convention of an omniscient author is philosophically unsound.

However powerful the impression of dream or pure mindstream the new novel may induce, we know that we are dealing with an art rather than with automatic writing or a literal tran-

[29] "François Mauriac and Freedom," *Literary and Philosophical Essays* (Criterion Books, 1955), p. 23.

scription of psychic experience. To simulate the processes of consciousness, as well as to obtain esthetic unity, it has borrowed heavily from the other arts. Musicians, for example, might see a sort of contrapuntal arrangement in the way episodes or scenes belonging to quite different periods of time are juxtaposed. They might see the recurrent scenes as themes with variations or as motifs. In his painstaking analysis of *Jealousy*, Professor Bruce Morrissette makes this point: "During the 'time' of the novel the protagonist observes, lives, suffers, and remembers the events of the plot, and makes of them, through his dynamic imagination, the 'experience' which is the novel itself. The result is a great formal freedom (variations of scenes, reiterations of themes with shifting emphasis, developments of episodes, metamorphoses of external elements and objects, etc.) bearing an analogy to musical structure . . ." [30] The orchestration of Robbe-Grillet's other novels could be studied with great profit, and for all the new novels a structural analysis in terms of music would be extremely illuminating. In a recent issue of *Yale French Studies*, Professor Kneller has studied *Moderato Cantabile*,[31] and I daresay someone will soon focus this attention on the works of Claude Simon, who presents his tableaux in an extremely interesting musical design.

Simon himself refers to painting rather than to music in explaining his composition, and one remembers that he was a painter before a writer and that the subtitle of *The Wind* (in the original) is "An Attempt at Restoration of a Baroque Retable." He professes to distinguish his personages and his themes by using colored inks for each, as a painter would. *The Flanders Road*, Simon disclosed to a reporter,[32] is designed after the club of playing cards, to draw which one crosses the same point three times. In the novel, this point is where the horsemen come three times upon the cadaver of a horse. Simon's confidences lead us to think that others among the new novelists may also have conceived of their works somewhat as paintings, with design and color

[30] "New Structure in the Novel: *Jealousy* by Alain Robbe-Grillet," *Evergreen Review*, III, 10 (November–December, 1959), 105.
[31] John W. Kneller, "Elective Empathies and Classical Affinities," *Yale French Studies*, 27 (Spring–Summer, 1961), pp. 114–120.
[32] Madeleine Chapsal, "Entretien avec Claude Simon," *Express*, November 10, 1960.

arrangement worked out on the principle of organizing a canvas
—Beckett, who is said to use colored pencils or pens too; Butor,
whose interest in the beaux-arts makes his text read at times like a
museum catalogue; and Robbe-Grillet, who builds a novel around
a picture (*In the Labyrinth*).

From the cinema there are unquestionable borrowings.
Expressions such as "close-up," "fade-out," and "montage" very
well describe composition techniques in a work of Robbe-Grillet
or Michel Butor. Consider the "shots" with which Robbe-Grillet
opens his novels—the café scene in *The Erasers,* the arrival of
the ferryboat in *The Voyeur,* the gradual exposure of the setting
and the characters in *Jealousy.* The style of the last named novel
with its flat, jerky sentences in the present tense reminds one
strongly of a scenario. Shots, close-ups, "followings" as the
character moves, fade-outs, and cuts—Robbe-Grillet composes
his scenes as if he were actually working with a camera. If the
mind of his character wanders back to former scenes, there are
flash-backs to present them. Devices suggestive of montage bring
the disparate elements of the narrative together. In *The Erasers,*
shots in which Wallas figures crisscross with those of police head-
quarters, of the clinic, of the Dupont house. Butor's *Passage de
Milan* is constructed on a pattern very familiar in the movies—
that of simultaneous scenes. The author's cameras are placed all
over the apartment house so that he can film what is going on in
various places at the same time. He composes, as it were, by cutting and assembling reels of film to achieve a sort of "Grand
Hotel" effect. The interest in the cinema and its techniques is very
strong among the youthful, modern-minded new novelists and it is
not surprising to see them turn, like Robbe-Grillet and Duras,
to actual scenario writing.

But it must be remembered that, in their novels, although
the new writers use structural devices inspired by the films, they
do so because it serves their literary aims. Musical composition or
scenario composition or any borrowing from other arts should
not be thought of as a *tour de force* or as an end in itself. The
novelists are not trying to turn the novel into a movie or a paint-

ing or a piece of music. Only, having renounced plot and action, they must seek in formal patterns the means of giving their works motor force and unity.

The obligation of formal patterns imposed by stream-of-consciousness writing has been pointed out by Robert Humphrey,[33] who classifies them:

1. The unities (time, place, character, and action)
2. Leitmotifs
3. Previously established literary patterns (burlesques and parodies)
4. Symbolic structures
5. Formal scenic arrangements
6. Natural cyclical schemes (seasons, tides, etc.)
7. Theoretical cyclical schemes (musical structures, cycles of history, etc.)

Professor Humphrey based his research upon Joyce, Woolf, and others writing in English, but it is clear that the new French writers avail themselves of the same patterns. They observe the unities quite rigorously to provide their works with a firm basic architecture. We have already noted the unity of time. Just as strict is the unity of space—a town, an island, a beach, a building, a veranda—but, as with time, not absolutely confining because of the mind's ability to liberate itself from the present place as well as from the present moment. The unity of character is maintained, not only by the relatively few personages involved (Duras and Beckett have reached the minimum) but also by close adherence to the single point of view. What passes for action is also narrowly confined—a trip, a sojourn, a mission, etc.

To illustrate how the new French writers use the formal devices listed by Humphrey, we have an embarrassment of riches: to do more here than make some brief indications and recapitulations is out of the question. Just a study of Robbe-Grillet's leitmotifs, beginning with the erasers in his first book, would constitute a monograph in itself. So would a study of symbolic

[33] *Stream of Consciousness in the Modern Novel* (University of California, 1954), p. 86.

structure, notably the widespread use of the quest or odyssey. Although it may well be considered to be based upon a "previously established literary pattern," the quest, as used by the French novelists, is generally not so specifically allusive as Joyce's *Ulysses*. Exception should be made for *The Erasers*, which is directly tied to the Oedipus story, for *Passing Time*, linked to the Theseus myth, and perhaps for Cayrol's story of Armand, which some see as a modern *Graal* epic. The detective story modification of the quest pattern is unquestionably an imitation, although to call such a work as *Portrait of a Man Unknown* a parody of the detective story is stretching the term a bit. In his introduction to Sarraute's work, Sartre called it that. None of the major new novels qualify as a real parody, and the burlesque element found in Joyce cannot be discovered in the French works on anywhere near the same scale. But several minor works might qualify: *Les petites Lecocq* of Hélène Bessette, which could be thought of as a mock village idyll; *Le Pire* of Lagrolet, which is a sort of fairy tale; and Pinget's works prior to *Monsieur Levert*, which are comic imitations.

The prominence given to city streets in the new novel has already been noted. They provide the "formal scenic arrangement" for the symbolic peregrinations found in Sartre, Butor, Robbe-Grillet, and Ollier. The beach is used by Marguerite Duras to give an effect of endlessness, the dimension of infinity, to her stories. For the opposite effect of confinement and oppresive immobility, Sarraute and Beckett place their heroes in the symbolic setting of small rooms or bedchambers. Utilization of the sort of scheme Humphrey refers to as cyclical can be amply demonstrated, particularly in the techniques reminiscent of other arts. Besides the "theoretical," moreover, some use is made of the "natural" cyclical scheme. We think of Claude Simon's *The Grass*—the old woman is dying, Sabine is getting old in spite of grotesque, frenzied efforts, her husband has become a mountain of flesh, while outside the grass continues to grow and in the orchard the pears rot beneath the trees. Relentless time and the processes of decay which victimize the household are repeated in the nature which surrounds them. Simon owes much to Faulkner, and his handling of the decay theme in *The Grass* suggests an interesting comparison with what Faulkner does to show the disintegration of Mississippi families, particularly in *The Sound and the Fury*. But differing from Faulkner and from the English stream-of-consciousness writers, from whom these narrative devices were borrowed, the new French writers have, at least more patently, a philosophical objective in mind. Formal patterns are for them actually more than the means of endowing their works with esthetic significance or even of depicting the processes of the psyche and the human adventure on earth. By using formal patterns to present life in the novel, the new writers further an ulterior purpose dear to their hearts—that of undermining the notions of chronology, of causality, and all the other props of the common-sense universe.

*Style and Syntax, Dialogue*

Style and syntax must, just like composition, be regarded in the light of the new novelists' philosophical repudiations. To replace language aimed at creating the realistic illusion, ordinary discourse with its orderly development and neat conclusions, each author has sought an expression suitable to his objective and faithful to his own vision of things.

The word vision is particularly fitting since description figures so prominently in the new novel. Its adepts were said by Emile Henriot to constitute an "école du regard," one remembers, and with writers like Butor, Robbe-Grillet, and Ollier, style is indeed primarily a matter of description. The reason for this emphasis on description is already clear: the novelist's notion of himself as chiefly a recording consciousness reduces him to a sort of seeing eye roving about the surface of things. One could well say a camera, as far as physical description goes; for, just as the organization of the new novel reminds one of films, most of the description, presented objectively, that is to say, in tableaux where conceptual knowledge is not permitted to modify the data presented by the eye, resembles what one sees at the movies. Hence descriptions are partial, selective, with proportions dictated by the limitations of the camera, the eye, or the preoccupation of the consciousness behind the eye. The apparently fortuitous descriptions of Robbe-Grillet have caused considerable comment. Maurice Nadeau, for example, maliciously suggests that to fill out a thin story the author just goes around with a ruler.[34] On the contrary, it is the mind which is apt to go around with a ruler, and any verbatim recording of consciousness would reveal the sort of apparently arbitrary attention to things, the scrutiny of trivia that Robbe-Grillet performs. The result is some curious descriptions like camera angles on planes and surfaces, or close-ups such as one of a tomato wedge in *The Erasers*, which might be used to illustrate a botany lesson. Michel Butor is merely following the vagaries of consciousness when he concentrates his gaze on the inscription of a train window and records the warning printed in three languages not to lean out. Such attention to minutiae may make quite tiresome reading; on the other hand, it may result in some lovely still-life painting or photography. In either case, it is an inevitable feature of an art which aims to present as authentically as possible the world as it appears to the eye of the narrator.

With each author committed to this aim, individual differences in description will be less a question of technique than of temperament. To Robbe-Grillet's concern for simple planes and surfaces, one can contrast Butor's interest in complicated and minutely wrought designs, whether they be of an insect fixed in amber or of a cathedral carving. Butor's books are like those European museums and galleries he is fond of visiting with his readers, full to the rafters of the most painstaking and minute word-painting, as if there were nothing he could leave out. His descriptions often have a lyrical, even rhapsodical quality that Robbe-Grillet's do not. *Passing Time* contains many poetic evocations of the city—nocturnes and twilight scenes, in which

[34] "Nouvelles formules pour le roman," *Critique*, August–September, 1957, p. 713.

Butor, with almost an oriental brush, paints lights glimmering through the rain.

Robbe-Grillet's mathematical descriptions are almost wholly visual and limited to form and line. Claude Ollier's are likewise of this sort. An accurate comparison of each author's imagery would entail a thorough investigation, but Butor's imagery gives the impression of being richer and more varied than either Robbe-Grillet's or that of his disciple, Claude Ollier. No richer or more varied, however, than Claude Simon's, whose descriptions are certainly the most lush of any to be found in the new novels. In contrast to Robbe-Grillet and Butor who, like Sartre and Cayrol, limit themselves mainly to towns, Claude Simon likes country settings in which he can frame his characters with nature. Trees, grass, flowers grow in profusion in his novels, providing a wealth of sensorial appeal. In this respect he is the most Faulknerian of the new French writers. Sartrian, on the other hand, best describes Nathalie Sarraute's imagery, for much of it tends towards the slimy and squashy sort that we find in *Nausea* and Sartre's other novels. Dealing with the lowest layers of psychological life, she presents her characters in terms we associate with protozoan or vermicious creatures. The impression is one of a sustained metaphor throughout her works, human responses being continuously turned into tropisms, which is the title she chose for her first book.

To speak of metaphor, however, in connection with the new writing is a little risky and one must immediately qualify. Sarraute would not consider her writing metaphorical and would be suspicious of the connotation the word metaphor has acquired, either the connotation of stylistic embellishment or that of being a key to the mysteries of the universe. There can be no question with the new writers of self-conscious elegance of style, nor do any of them subscribe to the mystic belief held by Proust and the symbolists that the metaphor constitutes the essential element of all literary art. Moreover, the tableau technique commonly employed in their description is too direct and photographic to invite allusive language. The only new writer who seems much given to figures of style is Claude Simon, whose heavily sensorial writing is frequently enhanced by simile and allusion. Michel Butor and Claude Ollier use figures more rarely and with great discretion. Robbe-Grillet has openly repudiated the metaphor. In his article "Old 'Values' and the New Novel" he declares that metaphor is never "innocent." By this he means that the assumption that the metaphor reflects or suggests fundamental analogies in nature tends to keep man in his fond error of considering that the universe possesses an inner unity and a soul with which the human soul is somehow in communion. For Robbe-Grillet, the surface of things is enough, and he avoids attributing to them values or qualities—particularly those suggesting kinship with humanity—that do not meet the eye: "To say that time is 'capricious' or a mountain 'majestic,' to speak of the 'heart' of the forest, of a 'pitiless' sun, of a village 'crouching' in the hollow of a valley . . . What loss would the village suffer if it were merely 'situated' in the hollow of the valley?" [35] The inspiration for Robbe-Grillet's thought may be found in Sartre, who, in his essay on Camus' *The Outsider*, had already written: "A nineteenth-century naturalist would have written 'A bridge spanned the river.' M. Camus will have none of this anthropomorphism. He says 'Over the river was a bridge.' " [36]

Syntactical patterns in the new novel vary considerably, not only between one writer and another but between the various narrative modes a given author is following. In straight description we find little out of the ordinary. Robbe-Grillet's writing is not marked by eccentricities of syntax, chiefly because the bulk of it is descriptive in nature. Whether a scene viewed or remembered, it is presented in sentence patterns as forthright and banal as a report. Even Butor's enumerations are unique only in their length. Where we find unorthodox syntax is in writing aimed at stream-of-consciousness imitation or in the interior monologue. Claude Simon's writing moves along like the inchoate flow of image and thought that makes up the mind-stream—he may continue over a page or more before halting the flow by a

[35] Robbe-Grillet, "Old 'Values' and the New Novel," *Evergreen Review*, III, 9 (Summer, 1959), 101–102.
[36] *Literary and Philosophical Essays* (Criterion Books, 1955), p. 39.

period. The period is a pause, not a logical conclusion, and the phrases that make up the sentence (if it can be properly called one) are loose aggregates without proportional relationships. Kateb Yacine, too, favors this sort of sentence in his slurred and simultaneous narrations and evocations which simulate the mind-stream. Butor's interior monologues are composed of interminable sentences often strung on a series of parallel secondary clauses which proliferate to the point of freeing themselves from the stem clause. The reader has considerable backtracking to do if he wishes to relate the parts of the sentence. Among the new writers, Simon and Butor give the strongest impression of verbal density and complexity, even more so than Beckett or Pinget, who also model their style directly on consciousness. Beckett marks, however, the extreme limit which the monologue can reach in its flight from normal logical prose, joined in one instance by Pinget, whose hero expresses himself finally in gibberish.

Dialogue has traditionally constituted one of the most important devices of novelists, for, alternating with direct exposition, narration, and description, it exhibits the character of the personages and keeps the story moving. However, when novelists present directly what is going on in the minds of their personages, they tend to rely less on dialogue to accomplish their ends and develop instead the techniques of stream-of-consciousness recording and the interior monologue. Thus in Robbe-Grillet and Butor, as in Jean-Paul Sartre before them, the protagonists keep rather much to themselves and their own thoughts. The new novelists are aware, nonetheless, of the possibilities that exist in dialogue to serve them, and some among them have exploited it to the full.

In writers like Simon, Lagrolet, and Cayrol, thoughts and emotions are simply exteriorized into conversation. It is difficult to tell, in *The Flanders Road*, for example, which is interior monologue and which is dialogue, so abruptly does Simon move from one technique to the other. The author tells the story, the characters chat among themselves, reminisce, relive episodes, spin yarns for each other outloud, half-outloud, or in their own heads—only rarely does a clearly indicated conversational exchange emerge from the unpunctuated mass of the novel. Lagrolet's personages appear to be conversing with their inner thoughts, with nothing of the reserve or the inhibitions which control dialogue in life. There is a dinner scene in *Les Vainqueurs du Jaloux,* which, judged by standards of polite intercourse, sounds like a party of lunatics. This is far from the realistic concept of dialogue, which, if not verbatim conversation, at least aimed to appear so. Of course the new novelists are not interested in creating the illusion of external reality. One would say, on the contrary, that they deliberately prevent it from forming. Claude Simon goes so far as to question, after recording a speech, if it were ever pronounced, then nonchalantly comments that if not, it was meant, or, if not pronounced at that time, at another! Hélène Bessette uses dialogue almost constantly, but never the sort one could ever actually have heard. Jean Cayrol admits his dialogues are not real ones and explains why: "I try always to get at the essential, and that is why my dialogues are not, in reality, true dialogues." [37]

There are, however, dialogues in the new novel that do aim to reproduce real ones. Sartre had scored the pretensions of French novelists like Mauriac who sought to give realistic credibility to their dialogue yet made their characters more articulate than their equivalent in life would be and packed each of their speeches with significance. To the concise, stagelike dialogue of the French tradition, Sartre prefers the stammering and clumsy speeches he finds in Dostoievsky, Conrad, and Faulkner, where characters, struggling to express themselves, create a thousand misunderstandings as well as provide involuntary revelations. Nathalie Sarraute, who knows her Sartre and her foreign novelists too, has been the chief exponent of fictional dialogue as Sartre would have it. But no more than the others is she interested in creating the realistic illusion.

What Sarraute is after is to dramatize the difference

[37] André Bourin, Interview in *Les Nouvelles Littéraires,* April 2, 1959.

between the sentiments a character is experiencing and his "in-authentic" talk that goes on upon the surface. Her first book, as Sartre noted,[38] is largely given over to "babble": "And they talked, kept on talking, repeating the same things, turning them over, then turning them over again, one side then the other, kneading them, kneading them, ceaselessly rolling between their fingers this thankless and poor matter that they had extracted from their life (what they called 'life,' their domain), kneading it, stretching it, rolling it until it was nothing between their fingers but a little pile, a little gray lump."[39] All the while, underneath the "ritual exchange of commonplaces," there is another conversation going on which is made up of advancements and retreats, of fears, revulsions, surging hopes, desires to placate —what Sartre calls a "sub-conversation" in which "the [sucking] valves touch, lick and inhale one another."[40] They must talk, talk—like Beckett's characters, even though they have nothing to say and might rather be silent. Like Marguerite Duras' characters, too, who prattle incessantly without saying anything but nevertheless reveal themselves and communicate by a sort of re-fraction and underneath their babble.

Robbe-Grillet's occasional dialogue is made up ex-clusively of terse exchanges of social commonplaces. The detec-tive in *The Erasers* passes the time of day with people he en-counters; the salesman in *The Voyeur* does likewise. Yet in spite of their commonplace nature they do not produce an illusion of everyday reality. They sound more like fragments of conversa-tion that appear in dreams, rising, as they do, out of Robbe-Grillet's strange world of angles; and, recurring in odd sequence, they obtain a really hallucinatory effect. Often they suggest more than they say, but it is in *Jealousy* that Robbe-Grillet comes closest to Sarraute's interplay between conversation and sub-conversation. Here the banal observations, the routine remarks about a shopping trip or about a new book take on the quality of enigmatic signs and omens. Butor, Pinget, and Ollier present their

[38] Sarraute, *Portrait of a Man Unknown*, preface by Jean-Paul Sartre, p. xi.
[39] *Tropismes* (Editions de Minuit, 1957) p. 65.
[40] Sartre's preface, p. xii.

dialogue, too, as terse and commonplace exchanges. Yet they, too, produce an unreal, eerie quality like that of familiar objects in a surrealistic setting, suggestive of mysterious meanings and of much left unsaid.

Nathalie Sarraute discusses the problem of dialogue in her essay "Conversation et sous-conversation." [41] Quoting Henry Green, who remarked on the increasing importance of dialogue in the English novel, she points out that, in spite of its banality, the discourse of characters is the external expression of something going on within and can be of great utility to the novelist. In her eyes, Ivy Compton-Burnett, whose novels are all conversation, illustrates the great power of dialogue. Never really verbatim conversation, yet never false nor gratuitous, dialogue represents a combination of surface talk and inexplicit communication which renders character in an unexcelled fashion. Dialogue, we may summarize then, has an important place in the new novel, but is not the sort usually encountered. These writers do not bring their characters together periodically to advance the story and create lifelike atmosphere by having them converse. Conversation occurs as something floating on the surface of consciousness, trivial or inoffensive in appearance but indicative of mysterious activity beneath.

Marcel Proust, in a letter to his friend Mme. Straus,[42] remarks that all artists are obliged to forge for themselves a new language. As a matter of principle, by their philosophical and esthetic views, the new novelists are committed to a revolution in expression. But what Proust wanted to stress was that each artist should consider it his first duty to find a means of translating his own unique inner vision, and one can legitimately ask if creating a new language to comply with endorsed principles does not risk neglecting the inner vision and merely substituting one convention for another. Bernard Dort's remark apropos of the re-

[41] It appears in *L'Ere du Soupçon.*
[42] *Correspondance générale,* II, 231–232.

bellion against the "psychological" tradition reminds us of this danger: "In liquidating the old literary myth, Robbe-Grillet risks giving birth to just as pernicious a myth." [43]

M. Dort's fear is, however, exaggerated. The theory advanced by the new novel, however dogmatically and categorically it may be worded, remains an ideal. No one has ever followed it to the letter. Jean-Paul Sartre, although the source of the theory of the new novel, himself writes rather conventional prose. Robbe-Grillet's practice, by his own confession, has not been quite what he preaches. Marguerite Duras wavers between new writing and conventional fiction. In varying degrees, the drag exerted by established practices of fiction must be felt by all the new novelists. Moreover, they reserve the right to experiment. To mention but one point—the matter of tense, which is a fundamental of style. Although Sartre insisted that the novel should depict the everlasting becoming, and although the phenomenological objective presumes a blending of the past and the future into the present, the present tense has not been consistently adopted by the new novelists. Robbe-Grillet himself, if he uses the present tense in one work, will prefer the preterite for the next. Whatever the reason—backsliding, desire to experiment, intervention of other considerations such as compromises with reader in mind— the new novel has fairly well avoided the stereotype.

Interpreting theory as ideal rather than formula, the new novelists enjoy a freedom of self-expression at least as great as has ever existed in a genre known for broad tolerance, and have been able to set themselves before what Proust considered the essential obligation of artists—to render their own vision of things. Proof is the marked individuality of style that each of the new authors has maintained. Who could deny that a personal sensitivity and temperament, a personal *Weltanschauung,* lies behind Robbe-Grillet's cold and precise notations, Butor's massy enumerations and sweeps of lyricism, the tangle of Simon's imagery, Duras' phrases heavy with things unsaid, Yacine's purple tirades, and Beckett's demential wail? To turn Buffon's famous phrase

[43] "Sur les romans de Robbe-Grillet," *Les Temps Modernes,* June, 1957, p. 1999.

into a sense the author probably did not mean: "Style is the man himself!"

It is normal for critics to have misgivings about any avant-garde, particularly one as self-conscious and intellectual as the new novel. André Billy, the dean of French journalistic critics, still prophesies that the new novel will have the same fate as the pre-World War I movement known as unanimism.[44] Yet the individuality the new novelists demonstrate (in spite of basic objectives in common) should make the critics less fearful. The authors themselves have evolved with each book, and without predicting how they will end (Billy prays they will return to the "permanent and fundamental rules of art"), we can be sure they will increasingly impose themselves as more than mere adepts of a literary cult. With every year Robbe-Grillet, Butor, Sarraute, and Simon gain a wider public at home and abroad. Moreover, we can be sure that the novel of the future will be enriched by the principles of fiction they champion. With every year new writers rally to the cause, and the new novel promises to become just the novel. One of the newer writers, Marc Saporta, affirms in a recent article, "The novel of the future cannot be anything other than a synthesis of the conventional forms and the new techniques." [45]

Accordingly, as the new novelists become less sensational figures—as the newness wears off—we may expect more painstaking and objective critical studies of their works. Up to now, they have been taken a bit too lightly by the established critics, who tend to scoff, or taken perhaps too seriously by fervent young intellectuals, who have made them the pretext for philosophical disquisitions. It is likely that these modes of criticism will not monopolize the field much longer. The new French novel is already worthy of the sort of impartial, unemotional investigation and judgment towards which this brief survey, designed to introduce the new novelists to a foreign audience, has itself been aimed.

[44] "Du côté du 'nouveau roman,' " *Le Figaro*, September 13, 1961.
[45] "Pro-romans et pré-textes," *Preuves*, October, 1961, p. 32.

# GENERAL DISCUSSIONS
# OF THE NEW NOVEL

Albérès, René Marill. *L'Aventure intellectuelle du XX* siècle* (Albin Michel, 1959).

*Arguments*, February, 1958. "Le roman d'aujourd'hui."
Pingaud, Bernard. "Le roman et le miroir," pp. 2–5.
Audry, Colette. "Remarques sur l'article de Pingaud," pp. 5–6.
Barthes, Roland. "Il n'y a pas d'école Robbe-Grillet," pp. 6–8.
Duvignaud, Jean. "Le roman n'a pas besoin de lois," pp. 8–10.

Billy, André. "Gérard Bauër, défenseur de nouveaux romanciers," *Le Figaro Littéraire*, September 6, 1958.

Blanchot, Maurice. "Le roman, œuvre de mauvaise foi," *Les Temps Modernes*, April, 1947, pp. 1304–1317.

———. *Le Livre à venir* (Gallimard, 1959).

Bloch-Michel, Jean. "Nouveau roman et culture des masses," *Preuves*, March, 1961, pp. 17–28.

———. "Une littérature de l'ennui," *Preuves*, January, 1962, pp. 14–23.

Boisdeffre, Pierre de. *Une Histoire vivante de la littérature d'aujourd'hui* (Le Livre Contemporain, 1961).

Borchardt, Georges, ed. *New French Writing* (Grove Press, 1961).
Peyre, Henri. "Trends in the contemporary French novel," pp. 73–87.

Bosquet, Alain. "Roman d'avant-garde et anti-roman," *Preuves*, September, 1957, pp. 79–86.

Bourin, André. "Techniciens du roman," *Les Nouvelles Littéraires*, January 22, 1959.

Brée, Germaine. "The 'New Novel' in France," *The American Society Legion of Honor Magazine*, XXXI, 1 (1960), 33–43.

Delpech, Jeannine. "Le roman français 1959," *Plaisir de France*, August, 1959, pp. 2–6.

Dort, Bernard. "Des 'romans blancs,' " *Cahiers du Sud,* No 334 (April, 1956), pp. 347–348.

———. "Tentative de description," *Cahiers du Sud,* No 334 (April, 1956), pp. 355–364.

Erval, François. "Les années 50," *Express,* December 31, 1959.

*Esprit,* July–August, 1958. "Le nouveau roman."
    Magny, Olivier de. "Nouvelle littérature romanesque," pp. 3–17.
    ———. "Dix romanciers vus par la critique," pp. 18–53.
    Pingaud, Bernard. "L'Ecole du refus," pp. 55–59. Translated in *Yale French Studies,* 24 (Summer, 1959).
    Dreyfus, Dina. "De l'ascéticisme dans le roman," pp. 60–66.
    Howlett, Jacques. "Notes sur l'objet dans le roman," pp. 67–71.
    ———. "Les Tropismes de Nathalie Sarraute," p. 72.
    Luccioni, Gennie. "Marguerite Duras et le 'roman abstrait,' " pp. 73–76.
    Dort, Bernard. "Sur 'l'espace,' " pp. 77–82.
    Pingaud, Bernard. "Y a-t-il quelqu'un?" pp. 83–85.
    Howlett, Jacques. "Distance et personne dans quelques romans d'aujourd'hui," pp. 87–90.
    Pingaud, Bernard. "Je, vous, il," pp. 91–99.
    Dort, Bernard. "Des romans 'innocents'?" pp. 100–110. Translated in *Yale French Studies,* 24.
    Estang, Luc. "Lettre à un jeune romancier," pp. 111–119.

*International Literary Annual,* II (Criterion Books, 1959).
    Cooper, William. "Reflections on Some Aspects of the Experimental Novel," pp. 29–36.

Kanters, Robert. "Situation présente du 'nouveau roman,' " *Le Figaro Littéraire,* March 26, 1959.

LeSage, Laurent. "The New French Novel," *The Saturday Review,* May 13, 1961, pp. 24–26.

Mauriac, Claude. "Le nouveau roman? L'école de l'amitié . . . ," *Le Figaro,* July 23, 1958.

———. *L'Alittérature contemporaine* (Albin Michel, 1958). Translated as *New Literature* (Braziller, 1959).

Miller, J. Hilles. "The Anonymous Walkers," *The Nation,* April 23, 1960, pp. 351–354.

Molnar, Thomas. "The New French School of Object-Worshippers," *The Catholic World,* October, 1958, pp. 31–35.

Nadeau, Maurice. "Nouvelles formules pour le roman," *Critique,* August–September, 1957, pp. 707–722.

————. "Le jeune roman," *Les Lettres Nouvelles,* March 25, 1959, pp. 1–2.

Paris, Jean. "The New French Generation," *The American Society Legion of Honor Magazine,* XXXI, 1 (1960), 45–51.

Picon, Gaëtan. "Du roman expérimental," *Mercure de France,* June, 1957, pp. 300–304.

————. *Panorama de la nouvelle littérature française* (Gallimard, 1960).

Pingaud, Bernard. *Ecrivains d'aujourd'hui* (Grasset, 1960).

Rousseaux, André. *Littérature du XX<sup>e</sup> siècle,* VII (Albin Michel, 1961).

Saporta, Marc. "Pro-romans et pré-textes," *Preuves,* October, 1961, pp. 32–34.

Simon, Pierre-Henri. "Sur le sens de l'antiroman," *Preuves,* May, 1961, pp. 52–55.

*The Times Literary Supplement,* February 13, 1959, and October 13, 1961.
  "The anti-novel in France."
  "Waves in a teacup."

Thiébaut, Marcel. "Le 'nouveau roman,'" *La Revue de Paris,* October, 1958, pp. 140–148.

Weightman, J. G. "The French Neo-realists," *The Nation,* April 25, 1959, pp. 381–384.

*Yale French Studies,* 24 (Summer, 1959). "Midnight Novelists." Contains translations of Pingaud and Dort, as indicated above. Other pertinent articles included in bibliographies on individual authors.

AUTHORS | TEXTS

## SELECTED WORKS

*Murphy* (London: 1938). Translated into French and published by Borda in 1947; taken over by Editions de Minuit, 1953 (New York: Grove Press, 1957).

*Molloy* (Editions de Minuit, 1951). Translated by Patrick Bowles (Grove Press, 1955).

*Malone meurt* (Editions de Minuit, 1951). Translated by the author as *Malone Dies* (Grove Press, 1956).

*L'Innommable* (Editions de Minuit, 1953). Translated by the author as *The Unnamable* (Grove Press, 1958).

*Watt* (Olympia Press, 1953; Grove Press, 1959).

*Nouvelles et textes pour rien* (Editions de Minuit, 1955).

*Comment c'est* (Editions de Minuit, 1961).

# SAMUEL BECKETT

Born in Dublin in 1906, Samuel Beckett was educated at Trinity College. From 1928 to 1929 he served as *lecteur d'anglais* at the Ecole Normale Supérieure in Paris, then returned to his school in Dublin the following year as an assistant in French. Beckett's literary inspiration is primarily James Joyce, whom he knew personally. Although he began to write in English and published his first novel in London, he has preferred French for the bulk of his works and has published them in Paris. Since 1938 he has resided in France. At present he lives somewhere outside the capital and leads a life of austerity and isolation. Beckett owes his fame to the success of his play, *En attendant Godot* (1952). This work introduced him to a wide public, and it is as a playwright that he is known the world over. His nondramatic pieces, which interest us here, reflect the same temperament and exhibit the same unconventionality of form which mark his plays.

As a novelist, Beckett stands as a living link between the young French authors and the foreign master James Joyce, whom they all revere. Beckett's ghostly and grisly fictions, which parody the world and man's lot, derive quite clearly from Joyce and anticipate the sort of writing the new generation advocates. Whether the name is Murphy, Molloy, Moran, or Malone, the protagonist is always Everyman recounting the human adventure on earth. Depending on which name he goes by, he is closer or farther away from the term of life; but for him, existence has been a quest ending in nothing. Like the outsider-heroes of the new novel, he is—by circumstances or by his own volition—isolated from his fellow men, free in his solitude to record his sensations and to ruminate endlessly upon the suffering of mortals. The work of Beckett is one long cry of metaphysical despair, and in its utterance nothing is left of the novel we refer to as conventional. The reader can only make up a story for himself, because Beckett refuses to tell one. From *Murphy* on, Beckett has cast aside practically all the usual fictional devices to give place only to the monologue of a consciousness babbling more or less coherently. His work, representing the ultimate disintegration of human personality, marks as well the zero point in the reduction of the novel.

Beckett's novels are long monologues delivered by abject and preposterous creatures whose relationship to human beings is only caricatural. Immobile and bereft of most of their faculties, they can only babble, curse, or cackle, as they describe their present condition and their past in so far as they can perceive or recollect them. Beckett's grotesques are intended to be a demonstration of the human condition—they are victims of all the ills of the flesh and the spirit, and their very existence makes mockery of the human adventure on earth. As we read his several novels— all on the same theme—we may often be reminded of Lautréamont, from whom he could claim descent. His Molloys and his Malones seem like unheroic copies of Maldoror.

The humor we find in Beckett, although perhaps just Irish in origin, bears a strong affinity to Lautréamont's famous *humour noir*. In the pages quoted from *Molloy* it is directed at family relationships, a subject on which such jesting would seem most offensive and shocking. Yet particularly the candid perverseness of the father, as indicated in the second fragment, shocks less than it entertains. Doubtless Beckett's excessiveness in depicting man's condition keeps us from taking him seriously—just as, in another field, the Marquis de Sade's horrors cease to be horrors, so exaggerated do they become.

Besides for me the question did not arise, at the period I'm worming into now, I mean the question of whether to call her Ma, Mag or the Countess Caca, she having for countless years been as deaf as a post. I think she was quite incontinent, both of faeces and water, but a kind of prudishness made us avoid the subject when we met, and I could never be certain of it. In any case it can't have amounted to much, a few niggardly wetted goat-droppings every two or three days. The room smelt of ammonia, oh not merely of ammonia, but of ammonia, ammonia. She knew it was me, by my smell. Her shrunken hairy old face lit up, she was happy to smell me. She jabbered away with a rattle of dentures and most of the time didn't realize what she was saying. Anyone but myself would have been lost in this clattering gabble, which can only have stopped during her brief instants of unconsciousness. In any case I didn't come to listen to her. I got into communication with her by knocking on her skull. One knock meant yes, two no, three I don't know, four money, five goodbye. I was hard put to ram this code into her ruined and frantic understanding, but I did it, in the end. That she should confuse yes, no, I don't know and goodbye, was all the same to me, I confused them myself. But that she should associate the four knocks with anything but money was something to be avoided at all costs. During the period of training therefore, at the same time as I administered the four knocks on her skull, I stuck a bank-note under her nose or in her mouth. In the innocence of my heart! For she seemed to have lost, if not absolutely all notion of mensuration, at least the faculty of counting beyond two. It was too far for her, yes, the distance was too great, from one to four. By the time she came to the fourth knock she imagined she was only at the second, the first two having been erased from her memory as completely as if they had never been felt, though I don't quite see how something never felt can be erased from the memory, and yet it is a common occurrence. She must have thought I was saying no to her all the time, whereas nothing was further from my purpose. Enlightened by these considerations I looked for and finally found a more effective means of putting the idea of money into her head. This consisted in replacing the four knocks of my index-knuckle by one or more (according to my needs) thumps of the fist, on her skull. That she understood. In any case I didn't come for money. I took her money, but I didn't come for that. My mother. I don't think too harshly of her. I know she did all she could not to have me, except of course the one thing, and if she never succeeded in getting me unstuck, it was that fate had earmarked me for less compassionate sewers. But it was well-meant and that's enough for me. No it is not enough for me, but I give her credit, though she is my mother, for what she tried to do for me. And I forgive her for having jostled me a little in the first months and spoiled the only endurable, just endurable, period of my enormous history. And I also give her credit for not having done it again, thanks to me, or for having stopped in time, when she did. And if ever I'm reduced to looking for a meaning to my life, you never can tell, it's in that old mess I'll stick my nose to begin with, the mess of that poor old uniparous whore and myself the last of my foul brood, neither man nor beast.

MOLLOY | pp. 22–23.

And yet there I was whistling away while I stuffed into my haversack a minimum of effects, similar to those I had recommended to my son. I put on my old pepper-and-salt shooting-suit with the knee-breeches, stockings to match and a pair of stout black boots. I bent down, my hands on my buttocks, and looked at my legs. Knock-kneed and skeleton thin they made a poor show in this accoutrement, unknown locally I may add. But when I left at night, for a distant place, I wore it with pleasure, for the sake of comfort, though I looked a sight. All I needed was a butterfly-net to have vaguely the air of a country schoolmaster on convalescent leave. The heavy glittering black boots, which seemed to implore a pair of navy-blue serge trousers, gave the finishing blow to this get-up which otherwise might have appeared, to the uninformed, an example of well-bred bad taste. On my head, after mature hesitation, I decided to wear my straw boater, yellowed by the rain. It had lost its band, which gave it an appearance of inordinate height. I was tempted to take my black cloak, but finally rejected it in favour of a heavy massive-handled winter umbrella. The cloak is a serviceable garment and I had more than one. It leaves great freedom of movement to the arms and at the same time conceals them. And there are times when a cloak is so to speak indispensable. But the umbrella too has great merits. And if it had been winter, or even autumn, instead of summer, I might have taken both. I had already done so, with most gratifying results.

Dressed thus I could hardly hope to pass unseen. I did not wish to. Conspicuousness is the A B C of my profession. To call forth feelings of pity and indulgence, to be the butt of jeers and hilarity, is indispensable. So many vent-holes in the cask of secrets. On condition you cannot feel, nor denigrate, nor laugh. This state was mine at will. And then there was night.

My son could only embarrass me. He was like a thousand other boys of his age and condition. There is something about a father that discourages derision. Even grotesque he commands a certain respect. And when he is seen out with his young hopeful, whose face grows longer and longer and longer with every step, then no further work is possible. He is taken for a widower, the gaudiest colours are of no avail, rather make things worse, he finds himself saddled with a wife long since deceased, in child-bed as likely as not. And my antics would be viewed as the harmless effect of my widowhood, presumed to have unhinged my mind. I boiled with anger at the thought of him who had shackled me thus. If he had desired my failure he could not have devised a better means to it. If I could have reflected with my usual calm on the work I was required to do, it would perhaps have seemed of a nature more likely to benefit than to suffer by the presence of my son. But let us not go back on that. Perhaps I could pass him off as my assistant, or a mere nephew. I would forbid him to call me papa, or show me any sign of affection, in public, if he did not want to get one of those clouts he so dreaded.

MOLLOY|pp. 169–171.

In *Malone Dies*, an old derelict about to die muses over his past life. He begins by describing as best he can where he is now. His faculties are all dim, all worn out—except, of course, his ability to write. Readers of Beckett must always "suspend disbelief" on one point: they must be willing to believe that a person pitifully aged and infirm—often reduced to little more than a larval existence—can hold a pencil and write superbly:

Present state. This room seems to be mine. I can find no other explanation to my being left in it. All this time. Unless it be at the behest of one of the powers that be. That is hardly likely. Why should the powers have changed in their attitude towards me? It is better to adopt the simplest explanation, even if it is not simple, even if it does not explain very much. A bright light is not necessary, a taper is all one needs to live in strangeness, if it faithfully burns. Perhaps I came in for the room on the death of whoever was in it before me. I enquire no further in any case. It is not a room in a hospital, or in a madhouse, I can feel that. I have listened at different hours of the day and night and never heard anything suspicious or unusual, but always the peaceful sounds of men at large, getting up, lying down, preparing food, coming and going, weeping and laughing, or nothing at all, no sounds at all. And when I look out of the window it is clear to me, from certain signs, that I am not in a house of rest in any sense of the word. No, this is just a plain private room apparently, in what appears to be a plain ordinary house. I do not remember how I got here. In an ambulance perhaps, a vehicle of some kind certainly. One day I found myself here, in the bed. Having probably lost consciousness somewhere, I benefit by a hiatus in my recollections, not to be resumed until I recovered my senses, in this bed. As to the events that led up to my fainting and to which I can hardly have been oblivious, at the time, they have left no discernible trace, on my mind. But who has not experienced such lapses? They are common after drunkenness. I have often amused myself with trying to invent them, those same lost events. But without succeeding in amusing myself really. But what is the last thing I remember, I could start from there, before I came to my senses again here? That too is lost. I was walking certainly, all my life I have been walking, except the first few months and since I have been here. But at the end of the day I did not know where I had been or what my thoughts had been. What then could I be expected to remember, and with what? I remember a mood. My young days were more varied, such as they come back to me, in fits and starts. I did not know my way about so well then. I have lived in a kind of coma. The loss of consciousness for me was never any great loss. But perhaps I was stunned with a blow, on the head, in a forest perhaps, yes, now that I speak of a forest I vaguely remember a forest. All that belongs to the past. Now it is the present I must establish, before I am avenged. It is an ordinary room. I have little experience of rooms, but this one seems quite ordinary to me. The truth is, if I did not feel myself dying, I could well believe myself dead, expiating my sins, or in one of heaven's mansions. But I feel at last that the sands are running out, which would not be the case if I were in heaven, or in hell. Beyond the grave, the sensation of being beyond the grave was stronger with me six months ago. Had it been foretold to me that one day I should feel myself living as I do to-day, I should have smiled. It would not have been noticed, but I would have known I was smiling. I remember them well, these last few days, they have left me more memories than the thirty thousand odd that went before. The reverse would have been less surprising. When I have completed my inventory, if my death is not ready for me then, I shall write my memoirs. That's funny, I have made a joke. No matter. There is a cupboard I have never looked into. My possessions are in a corner, in a little heap. With my long stick I can rummage in them, draw them to me, send them back. My bed is by the window. I lie turned towards it most of the time. I see roofs and sky, a glimpse of street too, if I crane. I do not see any fields or hills. And yet they are near. But are they near? I don't know. I do not see the sea either, but I hear it when it is high. I can see into a room of the house across the way. Queer things go on there sometimes, people are queer. Perhaps these are abnormal. They must see me too, my big shaggy head up against the window-pane. I never had so much hair as now, nor so long, I say it without fear of contradiction. But at night they do not see me, for I never have a light. I have studied the stars a little here. But I cannot find my way about among them. Gazing at them one night I suddenly saw myself in London. Is it possible I got as far as London? And what have stars to do with that city? The moon on the other hand has grown familiar, I am well familiar now with her changes of aspect and orbit, I know more or less the hours of the night when I may look for her in the sky and the nights when she will not come. What else? The clouds. They are varied, very varied. And all sorts of birds. They come and perch on the window-sill, asking for food! It is touching. They rap on the window-pane, with their beaks. I never give them anything. But they still come. What are they waiting for? They are

not vultures. Not only am I left here, but I am looked after! This is how
it is done now. The door half opens, a hand puts a dish on the little table
left there for that purpose, takes away the dish of the previous day, and
the door closes again. This is done for me every day, at the same time
probably. When I want to eat I hook the table with my stick and draw it
to me. It is on castors, it comes squeaking and lurching towards me.
When I need it no longer I send it back to its place by the door. It is soup.
They must know I am toothless. I eat it one time out of two, out of three,
on an average. When my chamber-pot is full I put it on the table beside
the dish. Then I go twenty-four hours without a pot. No, I have two pots.
They have thought of everything. I am naked in the bed, in the blankets,
whose number I increase and diminish as the seasons come and go. I am
never hot, never cold. I don't wash, but I don't get dirty. If I get dirty
somewhere I rub the part with my finger wet with spittle. What matters is
to eat and excrete. Dish and pot, dish and pot, these are the poles.

MALONE DIES|pp. 5–7.


REFERENCES

Nadeau, Maurice. "Samuel Beckett ou le droit au silence," *Les Temps
Modernes,* January, 1952, pp. 1273–1282.

Mackworth, Cecily. "Les Coupables," *Twentieth Century,* May, 1957, pp.
459–468.

Dreyfus, Dina. "Vraies et fausses énigmes," *Mercure de France,* October,
1957, pp. 268–285.

Mauriac, Claude, *L'Alittérature contemporaine* (Albin Michel, 1958).
Translated as *New Literature* (Braziller, 1959).

Brooke-Rose, Christine. "Samuel Beckett and the anti-novel," *London
Magazine,* December, 1958, pp. 38–46.

Tindall, William York. "Beckett's Bums," *Critique, Studies in Modern
Fiction,* II, 1 (1958), 3–15.

Blanchot, Maurice. "Where now? Who now?" *Evergreen Review,* VII, 2
(Winter, 1959), 222–229.

———. *Le Livre à venir* (Gallimard, 1959).

Cohn, Ruby. "Still Novel," *Yale French Studies,* 24 (Summer, 1959), pp.
48–53.

Cohn, Ruby. "A Checklist of Beckett Criticism," *Perspective* (Special Number, Autumn, 1959), pp. 193–196. Other articles on Beckett cover pp. 118–193.

Fowlie, Wallace. *Dionysus in Paris* (Meridian Books, 1960).

Friedman, Melvin J. "The Novels of Samuel Beckett," *Comparative Literature* (Winter, 1960), pp. 47–58.

————. "Samuel Beckett and the Nouveau Roman," *Wisconsin Studies in Contemporary Literature*, I, 2 (1960), 22–36.

Pingaud, Bernard. *Ecrivains d'aujourd'hui* (Grasset, 1960).

Blanzot, Jean. "Les romans de Samuel Beckett," *Le Figaro Littéraire,* May 13, 1961.

# SELECTED WORKS

*Lili pleure* (Gallimard, 1953).

*Materna* (Gallimard, 1954).

*Vingt minutes de silence* (Gallimard, 1955).

*Les petites Lecocq* (Gallimard, 1955).

*La Tour* (Gallimard, 1959).

*La Route bleue* (Gallimard, 1960).

# HÉLÈNE BESSETTE

Madame Bessette's *vita* not being readily available, the following information, sent on by her publishers, presumably comes from the author herself. I take the liberty of paraphrasing this highly personal account of a rich life and career. Hélène Bessette was born "obscurely" (as she puts it) in Levallois. After studying at a normal school, she married a preacher and, imbued with a fervent evangelical spirit, aided her spouse in propagating the faith in New Caledonia. Her fervor cooling considerably with the years, she abandoned her calling, her husband and two children. Apparently she returned to collect one of the children, however, for she speaks of her arrival back in France in 1950 with a suitcase of worn clothing, 1500 borrowed francs, and a young boy. Quite reluctantly she took up teaching, occupying at present a post in Eure-et-Loire.

Her writing career dates from the years in New Caledonia, where she launched a little Protestant paper, successful, we understand, "dans le genre." Her publications in volume began only after her return from the Pacific. They are all slight, sketchy bits made up of fragments of dialogue, silent film captions, and doggerel. Through them we can usually glimpse a story, say a little village idyll as in *Les petites Lecocq* or *Lili pleure,* but only through irony or the brusque humor produced by her unusual narrative devices. The introduction to *Materna,* vaguely about a primary school and its teachers, initiates the reader into the features of Mme. Bessette's style:

Novel without landscape.

No décor.

No time to decorate.

Without decoration.

Century of speed.

The reader is rushed.

The writer is rushed.

For her radical departure from conventional methods of writing a novel, her name is justifiably listed with the practitioners of the new novel. Her literary standing is somewhat dubious, however. Witness the scathing condemnation by Pierre de Boisdeffre: "A few critics have hailed Hélène Bessette as a genius from her first 'novel': but this lettrism [1] in the novel, this bowel-rumbling and onomatopoetic writing belongs to the worst sort of artifice." [2]

Hélène Bessette's are what one might call "do-it-yourself" novels—the author furnishes the materials, it is up to the reader to make something out of them. She gives him scenes, situations, dialogues in abundance—enough for a novel or a movie—but she herself claims to be too busy to sort or arrange. If one is in the mood to rise to the challenge, the technique can be very effective.

In *La Tour*, Mme. Bessette is as rushed and as bubbly as ever. Her theme is the young couple of today in their breakneck race after happiness, the happiness of "status," creature comforts, and gadgets—the sort spelled out in big letters by flashing neon signs and billboards, the sort promised overnight by lotteries and quiz programs. We are given glimpses of Louise and Marcel at each milestone as they push on and on. In the passage before us, they are somewhere near the half-way mark. It is typical of the author's presentation—a snapshot or a sketch created by a few brief strokes, free play of verbal associations, games of variants or synonyms, patterned syntactical and typographical effects, unusual diction.

Louise and Marcel fill the room with the passion of an unforgettable hour. Faces crack, split under the fire of glances. Disorder of movements. Clumsiness. Misunderstandings. Lapses. Errors. Fever of repartees. Blind one to the other. Money.

[1] *Le Lettrisme:* an absurd and unproductive French literary school founded in the late 1940's by one Jean-Isidore Isou, which championed nonsense verse.
[2] *Une Histoire vivante,* p. 427.

Gain. Getting ahead.

Years of life before and afterwards. Concentrated, condensed in a movement in time. The full life. Change possible. The strong savor of novelty. The overexcitement of curiosity. The satisfaction of the game well played. The unique conjunction of circumstances. It doesn't happen twice. Never again. Never renewed. Never before. Take it when you can. Don't lose the opportunity. Profit from the moment. The great joy of the unhoped for which arrives. The future becomes the present. The bronze laughter of good fortune that happens unexpectedly. The clash of cymbals. The gong with reverberating resonances. This day of life illuminated like a theater with indirect lighting.

Louise and Marcel, timid actors, self-conscious, dazzled. Scarcely knowing their parts. Floundering in their new role. That they dreamed of so much. That they worked up so much. That they hoped for so much. And,

When it arrives, finally,

after so many rebuffs. So many disappointments. So many dreams renounced. So many hidden tears. Between two slumbers. Between two nightmares. Between two vigils. Between two fatigues. After so many calculations come to naught. So many additions, multiplications unfinished.

When, finally,

this new role arrives, it finds them hesitating, unsure, badly prepared, stupefied, clumsy, unintelligent, nervous, fearful. Half-uttered laughs, uncertain.

Like disguised children. Not knowing what to do. On the edge of tears. Walk the wrong way. Half-executed gestures. Interrupted sentences. Restrained sobs.

Acquaintance with joy. Introduction to happiness. Hard is the encounter. Upsetting the meeting.

Louise, in a brief voice of rapid delivery, shrieks:

"What'll I wear? In your opinion, Marcel, what is most suitable?"

"I wouldn't know," he says, joyous, put out, preoccupied.

And grows pale against the knot of an extravagant and shimmering necktie.

LA TOUR|pp. 78–80.

REFERENCES

Bosquet, Alain. "Roman d'avant-garde et antiroman," *Preuves*, September, 1957, p. 86.

Boisdeffre, Pierre de. *Une Histoire vivante de la littérature d'aujourd'hui* (Le Livre Contemporain, 1961).

## SELECTED WORKS

*Thomas l'Obscur* (Gallimard, 1941).

*Aminadab* (Gallimard, 1942).

*Le Dernier Mot* (L'Age d'Or, 1947).

*Le Très-Haut* (Gallimard, 1948).

*L'Arrêt de Mort* (Gallimard, 1948).

*Thomas l'Obscur,* new version (Gallimard, 1950).

*Le Ressassement éternel* (Editions de Minuit, 1951).

*Au Moment voulu* (Gallimard, 1951).

*Celui qui ne m'accompagnait pas* (Gallimard, 1953).

*Le Dernier Homme* (Gallimard, 1957).

*L'Attente, L'Oubli* (Gallimard, 1962).

# MAURICE BLANCHOT

Maurice Blanchot, born September 22, 1907, in Quain (Saône-et-Loire), has been active in literary circles ever since completing his university studies. Journalist, novelist, critic—he is known best for his essays on the philosophy of literature. In recent years they have appeared regularly in the *Nouvelle Revue Française*.

We might call Blanchot the Mallarmé of the French novel, for he also is a writer in love with the absolute. His essays are long, meandering reflexions on language, its origins, its fundamental nature, and its possibilities. In a strange, esoteric fashion he links language with death, the essential and ultimate experience towards which all life tends. Language appears to him as a progression towards silence, the absolute speech. If Mallarmé's demon was that of analogy, Blanchot's is that of paradox. His thinking winds round and round upon itself until it seems that the essential antimonies of life and death, presence and absence, speech and silence resolve themselves into complete identity. In his criticism, he follows his metaphysical theme through other writers—English and German as well as French. In his creative pieces, he pursues it allegorically against a hallucinatory and fantastic background which recalls Kafka. *Aminadab,* which concerns a man who is seeking in a strange house the woman who has invited him there, would seem, for example, to depict humanity's groping efforts to orient itself in a world which it cannot understand. *Le Très-Haut* gives a vision of mankind at the end of history, thus anticipating the author's later ruminations on the last man on earth, the last writer, the meaningless buzz that occurs after the last word has been uttered.

The novel, as Blanchot makes use of it, is therefore primarily an investigation of the language phenomenon—its form becomes its content, so to speak. And just as he conceives of the word as destroying the object it represents, he conceives of novels which destroy the novel in all of its conventional attributes. His own hero is always a phantomlike Everyman who has no story, no situation, and indeed no character. He is there only as a witness to an absurd creation, as an intelligence striving after meaning, as a soul overwhelmed by a tragic sense of existence. In Blanchot's creative works, which fit so exactly Sartre's definition of the anti-novel, we can see already at work the corrosive agents which younger novelists continue to apply to the traditional structures of fiction.

In some sort of institution—a sanitarium, perhaps—one of the guests (or inmates) appears to be dying. This mysterious invalid is a constant preoccupation and subject of conversation for the narrator and a woman, apparently lovers, who live there too. The novel takes the form of a single monologue made up of the narrator's conjecture and musing, with bits of reported conversation and occasional allusion to event or situation worked in. Blanchot's usual themes of death and man's solitude sound throughout the work, rising in crescendo at the end to burst forth in an eerie apostrophe directed to a presence sensed by the narrator, to an ultimate interlocutor conceived of variously as a thought, a space, a calmness, a countenance—guises perhaps for God or Death, an alter ego, or the invalid friend. Blanchot's style, with its typical restraint on the one hand and, on the other, its metaphorical exuberance to depict mental states, can be judged from the following passage. One will note the recourse to paradox, a basic pattern in Blanchot's lucubrations.

If I reflect upon the event that took place, I should say that for me it almost merges with the calm that permits me to confront it. A gripping calm, quite near that word which was coming from so far off: not entirely to my measure, and even extraordinarily outside myself, but that did not bother me, I had my share in it, it touched me, it even pushed me back slightly as if to keep me on the edge of that moment where I would have to be calm.

I applied my thought to it, and although there was no real connection between us, I had the impression of a space to which I felt myself
linked by a wait, precautions, doubts, an intimacy, a solitude which
would have perhaps been appropriate for a living being: human? No, not
yet human, more exposed, less protected and however more important and
more real; but as this space was unknown to me, what linked me I
couldn't say. I only know that I owed it consideration, and even this I did
not know, for I owed it perhaps also a savage absence of consideration.

I had still another impression. This space, all the while seeming
infinitely distant and foreign, offered a means of immediate entry. It
seemed to me that if I succeeded in being calm, in being up to this calmness and in being within myself what it was outside of me, I would remain
in equilibrium not only with all my thoughts, but with the immobile, grave
and solitary thought, in the shelter of which mine continued to express
themselves so lightly.

It sufficed to wait. But to wait. . . . Had I taken the decisive
steps? Should I not concentrate more intensely on this very near event, by
which I felt I was being watched, through which I was doubtless watching myself, keeping watch over this calmness which was confided to my
negligence? And yet I was already enjoying, as if in spite of myself, this
new state. Never had I been so free, and my thoughts too, except that
grave, immobile thought, were freer, lighter, almost too light, giving me
over to a spirit of lightness that risked not leaving me long on a level with
myself. If I had wanted, I should have thought everything. But from that I
had particularly to keep myself—keep myself from the still more attrac-
tive impression that we were thinking everything, that all thought was
ours.

I shall not declare that this space was already clearly delimited,
but it could be, I felt, and it would be as soon as I entered it, at least
would perhaps be, a doubt remained. The doubt was powerful over each of
my steps, not only to push me back, but to make me go ahead. If it had
not been for a lack of certainty between it and me which protected us
both, if it had not been for my weakness, its own, my weakness so superior to me, so decided and so sure, I could not even have been able to
conceive of the thought vast enough to contain us both.

But I did not doubt the sort of presence that it constituted.
Since I had been there, I had been observing it, feeling it, leaning on it
lightly, my forehead leaning on my forehead, and what held me back was
that there was something too easy about this approach which left it without defense and me without resolution. It was too simple. What had held
me back for so long was perhaps that ease of it: a gesture and always
within reach. I could only remain astonished and hold back.

Something warned me that doubt must always be equal to certitude and certitude of the same nature as doubt.

It was necessary to wait, let it gather force by this wait,

strengthen its authority by contact with me and wear me out by this calm. It was necessary for it to find limits that would not be too foreign to my own, nor too strict either: let it close, but over me. Its instability, that is what frightened me suddenly, and yet I did not fear less a clarity which would have brought it too close to me. Familiar, it would have frightened me more than strange.

Everything was so calm that, were it not for the gentle, continuous pressure that it exerted on me, an extremely light and extremely firm pressure that I was not sure of not exercising on it by my resistance and by the direction of my waiting, I could have believed that I had already reached a certain goal—ultimate perhaps, one of the ultimate goals. However, the calm seemed also to place itself between us, not, it is true, like an obstacle, nor a distance, but like a memory.

A dangerous calm, I realized again, and as if a danger to itself, threatened, threatening, however unshakable, indestructible, it was definitive, a word that here appears opaque, but light.

It was dark, it was cold. The wait (the calm) gave me the feeling that over there, on one of the hillsides that I could situate only over there, there was an opening on a different region, still vainer and more hostile, that we both feared equally.

LE DERNIER HOMME│pp. 113–117.

In *Thomas l'Obscur*, the early novel which Blanchot reworked and presented again in 1950, each chapter begins in a deceptively realistic way with a few phrases in the manner of a *récit*. The initial sentences in Chapters I, II, III are respectively: "Thomas sat down and looked at the sea." "He decided however to turn his back on the sea and went into a small wood . . ." "He came back to the hotel for dinner." But each of these gambits is like a buoy to mark a dive into irreality and nightmare. On the surface of the novel we can make out the materials of a simple story—at least the characters and the setting: Thomas, a young man, and Anne, his fiancée; a summer hotel by the sea. But the plot plunges beneath the surface of light-of-day-happenings to relate hallucinations or oneiric experiences fancied as occurring in the limbos of death and annihilation. In the following Kafkaesque bit, a nightmarish vision of the death of the already dead, one notes again the important place of paradox among Blanchot's rhetorical processes.

Towards the middle of the second night, Thomas got up and went downstairs without a sound. No one noticed him but an almost blind cat which, seeing the night change form, ran behind this new night that he couldn't see. After having crept into a tunnel where he couldn't recognize a single odor, this cat began to meow, giving the deep-throated, raucous cry by which cats let you know that they are sacred animals. He swelled up and howled. He drew, from the idol that he became, the incomprehensible voice which addressed itself to the night and spoke.

"What's happening?" this voice said. "The spirits with whom I am usually in communication, the spirit that pulls my tail when the saucer is full, the spirit that picks me up in the morning and puts me to bed in comfortable eiderdown, and the spirit, the finest of all, the one that meows, purrs, and resembles me so much that he's like my own spirit, they've all disappeared. Where am I now? If I gently inspect with my paw, I don't find anything. There's nothing, anywhere. I'm on an eaves-trough farthest out, from which I can only fall. And it isn't falling that would frighten me. But the truth is that I cannot even fall; no fall is possible; I'm surrounded by a special void which pushes me back and which I don't know how to cross. Where am I then? Woe to me. Formerly, by suddenly turning into a beast that one could without qualms toss into the fire, I penetrated important secrets. I knew by a lightning flash that rent me in two, by the scratch that I gave, lies and crimes before they were committed. And now I'm a sightless creature. I hear a monstrous voice by which I say what I'm saying without understanding a single word of it. I think, and my thoughts are as useless to me as the grazing of fur and the contacts of ears would be to the foreign species to which I belong. Horror alone penetrates me. I turn round and round, uttering the lament of a frightful beast. I feel myself to be like a horrible sore, with a face as big as that of a spirit, with a smooth insipid tongue, the tongue of the blind, a deformed nose, incapable of presentiment, with enormous eyes lacking that straight flame that permits us to see the things within ourselves. My pelt is splitting. This is unquestionably the final operation. As soon as it's no longer possible, even in this night, to extract a supernatural light from me by rubbing my fur, it will be all over. I'm already darker than these shadows. I am the night of the night. I proceed, across shadows from which I can distinguish myself because I am their shadow, to meet the superior cat. No fear in me now. My body, which is altogether similar to a man's, the body of a blessed creature, has retained its dimensions, but my head is immense. A noise can be heard, a noise that I've never yet heard. A light that seems to be emerging from my body, although it is dim and damp, makes a circle around me that's like another body that I can't get out of. I'm beginning to distinguish a landscape. While the obscurity gets heavier, a big, whitish face rises before me. I say me, guided by a blind instinct, because since I lost the perfectly straight tail which served as my rudder in the world, I'm no longer manifestly myself. This head which is unceasingly growing and seems to be only a look instead of a head, exactly what is it? I don't see it without discomfort. It's moving, it's approaching. It's turned exactly towards me and, in spite of being nothing but a look, gives me the terrible impression of not perceiving me. This sensation is intolerable. If I still had fur, I would feel it stand on end all over my body. But, in my state, I don't even have the means of experiencing the fear that I feel. I'm dead, dead. This head, my head, doesn't even see me, because I'm annihilated. For, it is I who look at myself and cannot distinguish myself. Oh, superior cat that I became for an instant to verify my decease, now I'm going to disappear for good. First I cease to be a man. I become again a cold, uninhabitable little cat, stretched out on the ground. I howl one more time. I cast a last glance on that valley which is going to close up again and where I see a man, he too a superior cat. I hear him scratch the earth, probably with his claws. What they call the beyond is ended for me."

THOMAS L'OBSCUR|pp. 42–47.

REFERENCES

Sartre, Jean-Paul. *Situations* (Gallimard, 1947). Translated as *Literary and Philosophical Essays* (Criterion Books, 1955).

Poulet, Georges. "Maurice Blanchot as a Novelist," *Yale French Studies*, 8 (1951), pp. 77–81.

Lagrolet, Jean. "Nouveau réalisme?" *La Nef*, January, 1958, pp. 62–70.

Boisdeffre, Pierre de. *Une Histoire vivante de la littérature d'aujourd'hui.*

Pingaud, Bernard. *Ecrivains d'aujourd'hui.*

## SELECTED WORKS

*Passage de Milan* (Editions de Minuit, 1954).

*L'Emploi du temps* (Editions de Minuit, 1956). Translated by Jean Stewart as *Passing Time* (Simon & Schuster, 1960).

*La Modification* (Editions de Minuit, 1957). Translated by Jean Stewart as *Second Thoughts* (Faber, 1958) and as *A Change of Heart* (Simon & Schuster, 1959).

*Degrés* (Gallimard, 1960). Translated by Richard Howard as *Degrees* (Simon & Schuster, 1961).

*Histoire extraordinaire, essai sur un rêve de Baudelaire* (Gallimard, 1961).

*Mobile* (Gallimard, 1962).

"L'Ecriture pour moi est une colonne vertébrale," *Les Nouvelles Littéraires,* February 5, 1959.

"L'Usage des pronoms personnels dans le roman," *Les Temps Modernes,* February, 1961, pp. 936–948.

"Votre Faust," *La Nouvelle Revue Française,* January-February-March, 1962

Other articles collected in *Répertoire* (Editions de Minuit, 1960).

# MICHEL BUTOR

Born September 14, 1926, in Mons-en-Baroeul (Nord), a suburb of Lille, Michel Butor was taken to Paris at the age of three. After secondary and university studies (*licence* and *diplôme de philosophie*), he became a teacher. His positions have been at Sens, Minieh (Upper Egypt), Manchester, Salonica, and Geneva. Bryn Mawr invited him as visiting professor for the spring semester of 1960. Butor is married and makes his home in Paris.

Butor reached the novel by way of philosophy and poetry, his favorite studies as a student. While reading the philosophers, particularly the phenomenologists (subject of his Sorbonne thesis announced but never presented: "La Notion de l'ambiguïté en littérature et l'idée de signification"), he was also composing poems and methodically studying surrealists and English contemporary poets. The novel appeared to him the perfect means of combining his two interests—the phenomenological domain par excellence, where one can study how reality appears to us or how it can appear, and the modern vehicle for epic and didactic poetry.

*Passage de Milan,* his first novel, received little notice and uncertain appreciation, although one critic, Jean Mauduit, discerned in it the expression of a new Realism and associated it with Robbe-Grillet's work.[1] *La Modification (A Change of Heart)* put Butor before the general public, for this novel received one of the major French literary prizes of 1957. Henceforth Butor would figure prominently in French literary news, lecturing, writing articles and replying to interviews, appearing on the radio. Although he is closely associated with the advance guard movement, Butor has enjoyed greater popularity than any of the others. Critics have been more kindly disposed and the public, perhaps

[1] In the *Témoignage Chrétien* of May 14, 1954.

reassured by his conservative grooming and air of well-bred intelligence, have followed suit.

The stuff of Butor's novels is consciousness, frequently presented in the form of the interior monologue. His first effort was a novel of simultaneity, *Passage de Milan*, an account of an evening party in an apartment house, in which the author slips from one character to another, back and forth throughout the building from the concierge's loge to the servants' rooms under the roof, to keep track of what everyone is doing and thinking. What amounts in Butor to an obsession of totality, we encounter first here in his ambition to cover such a wide area. It does not make for easy reading. It is hard to keep the characters straight, remember just who is involved in which little drama on which floor, and when the novel ends with a murder, we groan that we have been served too much.

The next two novels spread themselves out less but cut more deeply. The reading is no less taxing. That is to say, by concentrating on one person in *L'Emploi du temps* (*Passing Time*) and *La Modification* (*A Change of Heart*), Butor gives us consciousness in such detail and at such length, keeps forever probing and examining at one spot that the effect is equally oppressive. In *Degrees*, he returns to the device of simultaneous consciousness while if anything concentrating on minutiae more, with the unhappy effect of producing both bewilderment and boredom.

*Passing Time* describes a year spent by a young Frenchman in a large English city. The journal he keeps is not only an account of each day's happenings and of his mood, but the record of his effort to make sense and reality out of what he experiences. Nothing must escape his scrutiny, pass by unrecorded. What is particularly important is that this journal is not a day-by-day jotting, but a record made months afterwards. Thus the novel moves on two temporal planes: the date on which the character is writing and the date he is recalling. It is not until May that Jacques Revel begins his desperate attempt not to let the past escape, and reconstructs his arrival in October. In the following passage, he describes the task he has set for himself.

Monday, May 19 This is where my real research begins; for all the incidents I have noted hitherto have often recurred to my memory during the past seven months, vivid and intact, belonging unmistakably to those first seven clearly differentiated days which form a quite separate period, a prelude, those days preceding October 8, the date on which I first embarked on the full week's round at Matthews and Sons in company with all my fellow workers and began to rotate with them, chained to that grindstone which, on this as on every other Monday morning at nine, has just resumed its unvarying motion, so that when I crossed the threshold of 62 White Street I might have been back in the past, a week ago, a fortnight ago, or even on that same October 8, the setting being always the same, varied only by a decrease of light until January and an increase of light afterward, with the same actors in the same attitudes, so that I should find it hard to specify at what moment some particular trivial incident occurred, even though this may have served for a long time as a topic for office chat at meal times, on meeting, or on parting (Ardwick's new suit, his first in five years, Greystone's bronchitis, Slade's mourning for his father's death, or an unforgettable display of temper by old Matthews, who had burst in with a handful of blank sheets of paper and torn them into shreds that had fluttered away and settled on all our desks, or the unexpected visit of his second son, William Matthews, the firm's London representative, or the breakdown of the central heating—"Wasn't it nice to see a coal fire in the grate, Monsieur Revel?"), so that in my memory all those weeks, the number of which appalls me when I consult my calendar, and each of which dragged by so slowly, seem to be contracted into a single immense week, a dense, compact, confused week, all that is left to me of that long autumn and winter and early spring, that unvarying motion which will not stop until the end of September, since I am not to take a holiday while I am here.

This is where my real research begins; for I will not rest content with this vague abridgment, I will not let myself be cheated of that past which, I well know, is not an empty past, since I can assess the distance that divides me from the man I was when I arrived, not only the extent to which I have been bogged down and bewildered and blinded but also the gains I have made in some areas, my progress in the knowledge of this town and its inhabitants, of its horror and its moments of beauty; for I must regain control of all those events which I feel swarming within me, make them fall into shape despite the mist that threatens to obliterate them, I must summon them before me one by one in their right order, so as to rescue them before they have completely foundered in that great morass of slimy dust, I must rescue my own territories foot by foot from the encroaching weeds that disfigure them, from the scummy waters that are rotting them and preventing them from producing anything but this brittle, sooty vegetation.

PASSING TIME|pp. 34–35.

*A Change of Heart* describes what is going on in a man's mind during a train trip from Paris to Rome. As manager of the French office of an Italian typewriter firm, he has made the trip many times. This time it is different, however, for he expects to announce to his mistress in Rome that he is leaving his wife. While dozing, looking out of the window, or observing other passengers, he lets his mind flit back to scenes and episodes which have brought him to this decision. When the train pulls in to the station, however, he has changed his mind.

In this novel, Butor's third, we recognize his usual photographic attention to detail and the syntactical peculiarities that mark his style. Long, complicated sentences extend over whole paragraphs—even more, frequently, by a trick of starting a new paragraph on an uncapitalized word or phrase picked up from a previous utterance. The paragraph that begins thus is a fragment, often requiring a hunt back through the text to find the source of the pivotal word or the initial part of the sentence. Sometimes a whole series of parallel paragraphs are strung out in this fashion. What is, however, unique in the technique of *A Change of Heart* is the substitution of the second person for the usual third or first person as the narrative agent. This gives the startling impression that the hero is addressing himself or that the author is making the reader the hero of his novel. Here are the opening paragraphs:

Standing with your left foot on the grooved brass sill, you try in vain with your right shoulder to push the sliding door a little wider open.

You edge your way in through the narrow opening, then you lift up your suitcase of bottle-green grained leather, the smallish suitcase of a man used to making long journeys, grasping the sticky handle with fingers that are hot from having carried even so light a weight so far, and you feel the muscles and tendons tense not only in your finger joints, the palm of your hand, your wrist and your arm, but in your shoulder too, all down one side of your back, along your vertebrae from neck to loins.

No, it's not merely the comparative earliness of the hour that makes you feel so unusually feeble, it's age, already trying to convince you of its domination over your body, although you have only just passed your forty-fifth birthday.

Your eyes are half closed and blurred with a faint haze, your eyelids tender and stiff, the skin over your temples drawn and puckered, your hair, which is growing thinner and grayer, imperceptibly to others but not to you, not to Henriette or Cécile or, nowadays, to the children, is somewhat disheveled, and your whole body feels ill at ease, constricted and weighed down by your clothes, and seems, in its half-awakened state, to be steeped in some frothing water full of suspended animalcula.

You have chosen this compartment because the corner seat facing the engine and next to the corridor is vacant, the very seat you would have got Marnal to reserve for you if there had still been time, not the seat you would have asked for yourself over the telephone, since nobody at Scabelli's must know that it's to Rome you are escaping for these few days.

A man on your right, his face level with your elbow, sitting opposite that place where you are going to settle down for this journey, a little younger than you, not over forty, taller than you, pale, with hair grayer than yours, with eyes blinking behind powerful lenses, with long restless hands, nails bitten and tobacco-stained, fingers crossing and uncrossing nervously as he waits impatiently for the train to start, the owner, in all probability, of that black briefcase crammed with files, a few colored corners of which you notice peeping through a burst seam, and of the bound and probably boring books stacked above him like an emblem, like a legend whose explanatory or enigmatic character is not lessened by its being a thing, not a mere word but a possession, lying on that square-holed metal rack and propped up against the partition next the corridor,

this man stares at you, irritated at your standing motionless and with your feet in the way of his feet; he would like to ask you to sit down, but his timid lips cannot even frame the words, and he turns towards the window, pushing aside with his forefinger the lowered blue shade with its woven initials SNCF.

On the same seat as this man, next to a space at present vacant but which someone has reserved with that long umbrella in its black silk sheath stretched against the green oilcloth, beneath that light attaché case in its waterproof tartan cover, with its two gleaming locks of thin brass, a fair young man who must just have finished his military service, dressed in light-gray tweed, with a diagonally striped red-and-purple tie, holds in his right hand the left hand of a young woman, darker than himself, and plays with it, passing his thumb to and fro across her palm while she watches him contentedly, raising his eyes for a moment to look at you and dropping them quickly when he sees you watching him, but without stopping his play.

They are not merely lovers but a young married couple, since they are each wearing a new gold ring, on their honeymoon perhaps, and they must have bought for the occasion, or else have been given by a generous uncle, those two big, identical pigskin cases, brand-new, one on top of the other above their heads, with little leather label frames fixed to the handles with tiny straps.

They are the only ones to have reserved their seats in this compartment; their brown-and-yellow tickets, with big black numbers on them, hang motionless from the nickel-plated rail.

On the opposite side of the window, sitting by himself on the other seat, an ecclesiastic of about thirty, already plumpish, meticulously clean except for the nicotine-stained fingers of his right hand, is trying to bury himself in his breviary, which is stuffed with pictures, while above him a briefcase, the grayish-black color of asphalt, with its zipper gaping a little like the needle-toothed jaw of a sea serpent, lies on the rack, onto which, straining, like some grotesque athlete at a fair lifting by its ring a huge, hollow cast-iron weight, and using one hand only since your other is still clutching the book you have just bought, you hoist your own luggage, your own suitcase of bottle-green, coarse-grained leather, stamped with your initials L.D., a present from your family on your previous birthday, which was really rather smart then and quite suitable for the head of the Paris office of Scabelli Typewriters, and which can still pass muster despite the grease spots revealed by a close scrutiny and the insidious rust that has attacked the hinges.

A CHANGE OF HEART|pp. 1–4.

*Degrees* is a novel about a novel. A lycée teacher begins by attempting to describe a class in which his own nephew, Pierre Eller, is a pupil. His idea is to present his composition to the boy, who will thereby have a permanent record of a moment in his life. But to capture the reality of the class he faces Herculean labor: the complex relations among the pupils, their past histories, their other classes, the other teachers, what they are doing in their classrooms. There is no stopping point either in time or space, for everything is inextricably bound up with everything else. Pierre

Vernier's search for the absolute puts him finally in the hospital (where he may have belonged all along), but in the data he has collected we glimpse some interesting situations—the intimate life of several of his colleagues, his own friendship with an understanding young woman, the interests and activities of schoolboys. All this would have made a good novel "à la Balzac," an epic of the French lycée. The conventional joys of novel reading are offered us begrudgingly, however, and we are indulged only as a reward for patiently following the manic lucubrations of the hero. To obtain the "reality" of the lycée, he must not limit himself to his own point of view, but pretend that he is another teacher, Henri Jouret, who is also Pierre Eller's uncle, and pretend also that he is their common nephew. Thus the narrative ostensibly passes from Pierre Vernier to Pierre Eller and to Henri Jouret. The following passage, typical of the notations that make up this novel, is curious for the ending in which the fiction of the nephew-author is deliberately destroyed. But for the moment young Pierre is supposed to be addressing his uncle.

The first question didn't give me too much difficulty, a line joining points of equal temperature, whether extremes or an average; all I could remember about the second was that the second coldest place was in Siberia, that the hottest place must be in the Sahara and similar deserts; but to find out what an inversion of temperature was, I had to look at what Michel Daval was writing next to me—he didn't know either—or what Alain Mouron was writing in front of me.

On Tuesday, Jacques was sick, another cough. He didn't go to school, stayed in bed, ate virtually nothing for lunch.

We each went in to talk to him a little, and you came to find out how he was and brought him some mint drops.

Then you told your seventh-graders about the Hebrews, their religion, their sacred books which constitute the Bible.

Uncle Henri gave us a new French assignment:

"What do you think of Rabelais' ideas about education? Compare today's education with the kind Rabelais opposes and the kind he proposes,"

to be handed in on Tuesday, November 9,

before making us read what we had had to prepare for that day, the praise of the marvelous herb called Pantagruelion, that is, hemp,

". . . without it, kitchens would be a disgrace, tables repellent . . ."

After that, Monsieur Bonnini made his seniors write out in class the translation of the passage from the *Purgatorio* about the Valley of the Princes; Michel Daval, beside me, was taking down from your dictation:

"The Scandinavian invasions."

There were three days' holiday for All Saints' Day; you took advantage of it to make considerable progress in the writing of this work and the study of our textbooks.

Consequently, on Tuesday afternoon, All Souls' Day, you reread Racine's *Iphigénie* which Uncle Henri was making his seniors study.

I was camping with the other patrol leaders on the grounds of a little Seine-et-Oise château. The rain had forced us to take refuge in an abandoned stable. There was a big shaky table, crates that we used as stools, an old wood stove on which we boiled water for tea.

The following week, the routine resumed without a hitch.

When you came into our classroom, you noticed the absence of Francis Hunter and Denis Régnier, you called on Rémy Orland about clouds and their various systems, François Nathan about rain and other forms of precipitation: fog, hail, dew, mist and snow.

The photographs illustrating the next lesson, climates and types of weather:

two views of the New Hebrides, one of Saint-Pierre-et-Miquelon: tiny house on the oblique horizon above dwarf pines, another taken in Mexico, a hedge of tall succulents like candles.

My brother Denis was sick in his turn, a good dose of grippe, beside his bed the phonograph he himself had assembled out of spare parts. It scratched a lot, but he was very proud of his handiwork and turned it up as loud as it would go. We could hear it in the dining room during lunch.

"He's going to wear himself out with all that noise."

"Let him alone, it's nice for him. As long as the neighbors don't complain . . ."

Coming up to get your books for the afternoon, you stopped to give him a little 45 repressing of Duke Ellington that delighted him and that he immediately tried on his machine; unfortunately something was wrong with the speeds. He stopped everything and started to take the machine apart, scattering parts all over the bed.

All of which interested me a lot, but it was time to go back to school, I ran, and passed you in the street, you were with Jacques.

On the way in, you gave me a wink. We had an appointment for after class, a reconnaissance meeting.

Written quiz for the seventh grade:

"What do you know about Crete?

What do you know about the Phoenicians?"

before telling them about the Homeric poems and in particular the travels of Ulysses. Claiming that it was to reward them for good conduct, you read them, in Victor Bérard's translation, Ulysses' arrival on the Island of the Phaeacians:

"But Pallas Athena then had her design . . ."

We handed in to Uncle Henri our composition on Rabelais' ideas of education; he told us about Calvin's life.

Now Monsieur Bonnini, dressed all in black, is continuing the reading of the *Purgatorio* with his seniors.

Michel Daval is drawing a pair of spectacles on Lebrun's portrait of Turenne.

I say now, but it isn't really now, just as I'm not actually doing the writing; that hour was over long ago, and this present tense I'm using is like the pier of a bridge connecting these other present tenses:

the one in which you are writing, the one in which I and my classmates will read you,

at that central hour which is becoming more and more remote and which you distinguish from all the rest, which surround it with ever-increasing density,

by utilizing it for a motionless present-tense narrative,

whereas for this particular hour, the middle of the afternoon of Tuesday, November 9, 1954, the next time you come back to it, focusing your mind on another student and another professor, since you will want to situate it, too, among other hours, not only after those which preceded it, but before those that have followed it,

you will make me describe it in the past.

DEGREES│pp. 162–164.

REFERENCES

Pouillon, Jean. "Les Règles du jeu," *Les Temps Modernes*, April, 1957, pp. 1591–1598.

Leiris, Michel. "Le Réalisme mythologique de Michel Butor," *Critique*, February, 1958, pp. 99–118.

Price, Martin. "The Difficulties of Commitment: *A Change of Heart*, by Michel Butor," *Yale Review*, June, 1959, pp. 598–599.

Frohock, W. M. "Introduction to Butor," *Yale French Studies*, 24 (Summer, 1959), pp. 54–61.

Pingaud, Bernard. *Ecrivains d'aujourd'hui.*

Deguise, Pierre. "Michel Butor et le 'nouveau roman,'" *The French Review*, December, 1961, pp. 155–162.

# SELECTED WORKS

*Je vivrai l'amour des autres* (Le Seuil)
I. *On vous parle*, 1947.
II. *Les premiers jours*, 1947.
III. *Le feu qui prend*, 1952.

*La Noire* (Le Seuil, 1948).

*Le Vent de la mémoire* (Le Seuil, 1951).

*L'Espace d'une nuit* (Le Seuil, 1954).

*Le Déménagement* (Le Seuil, 1956).

*La Gaffe* (Le Seuil, 1957).

*Les Corps étrangers* (Le Seuil, 1959). Translated by Richard Howard as *Foreign Bodies* (Putnam, 1960).

# JEAN CAYROL

Born in Bordeaux on June 6, 1911, Jean Cayrol lived in that city until World War II. He was educated in the humanities and in law; upon the completion of his studies he performed his military service in the navy. Subsequently he worked as a librarian. His literary career, begun before the war with the publication of two volumes of poetry, was halted during the occupation. He was arrested in 1942 for clandestine activities and spent the remaining war years as a deportee in Germany. After the liberation, Cayrol resumed his writing, publishing more poems and making a brilliant début in fiction with the first two tomes of his trilogy, *Je vivrai l'amour des autres*. He has since written novels steadily, continued to publish verse, and has brought out several essays as well. His fiction has consistently been published by Le Seuil, where Cayrol now works as a staff-member and editor of the review *Ecrire*.

Appearing as a novelist in the immediate postwar period, Cayrol was already firmly established before the new novel became a literary issue. However, critics of the new school have considered him a kindred spirit, which he is indeed by aspects of his technique, theme, and concept of the novel. His writing stands quite apart from the French sociological or psychological tradition, belonging rather to that of the *Entwicklungsroman,* the "duration" novel which Sartre and the new novelists all advocate. His hero moves blindly along in the adventure of his life, neither knowing where he is going nor ever really arriving. He is seeking something, his salvation perhaps, but all we can be sure of is that he will discover the world. The world for a man like Armand of *Je vivrai l'amour des autres* is the world of objects, that of banal mechanical miracles of city streets along which he wanders. Setting and structure of Cayrol's novels meet the specifications of the new novel; and his "Lazarian" themes—man's loneliness, his plight in a universe that fills him with awe and apprehension, his gropings to distinguish the true from the false, the real from the unreal—belong to the order of Existentialist and Phenomenonological preoccupations. Moreover, younger writers can find in Cayrol the approved fictional devices of monologue and the restricted point of view. Cayrol himself has never been dogmatic in novelistic theory, but has given his blessing to Robbe-Grillet and the new school, who quite rightly hail him as a master.

Gaspard, the monologist in Cayrol's first translated novel and a spiritual brother of all Cayrol's heroes, is telling his life. It is the life of an anonymous man of the city streets, child of the century, waif, and derelict. One gathers that Gaspard came originally from the farm, trafficked during the occupation, has lived since from hand to mouth, perhaps pimped a little, played stool pigeon, robbed occasionally, may even have committed murder. But one cannot be certain about details, because his story is full of lies, then repudiation of those lies, then more lies. The character emerges perfectly clear, however, from the confused yarn Gaspard spins, which, characteristic of the new novel, is invented as it goes along. Scrupulously maintaining the one point of view, the author never tells us directly more than his character, but Gaspard's denials are tantamount to confessions, as in the following passage:

It was no fault of mine if a dance-hall trumpet player had mentioned a consignment of bicycle brakes and headlights in public. I never wanted to get him arrested. But how indiscreet he was! He improvised, like his music. The night loosened his tongue, and he talked too much between sessions. Any music lover became his closest friend after two rounds of drinks.

The police realized I was innocent at once. Only how to prove it? I didn't like this German-American jazz player. He hovered over Claudette, murmuring something, annoying her with his greedy lips, his Pekinese eyes. He was pale, like all great artists. Besides, he coughed, which gave him an incontestable sickly charm. A poor slob who supported his mother with his miserable salary. It was a good thing he disappeared the way he came. The orchestra went on playing just as badly as before. I never went back to that dump—it smelled of greasy hair and its frenzy was routine. But I had to go to places like that: I could always pick up information useful to my business. It was ridiculous that Jews were forbidden to go to such places. No Jew would ever show up in such a stinking hole.

No one slapped me in that cheap little dance hall. People said I ran out with a handkerchief held to my cheek. That's not true . . .

FOREIGN BODIES│pp. 86–87.

If the hero tries continually to justify his actions, the author never does, except by the implied pathos of such an "existence manquée," which is a basic Cayrolian theme:

I didn't hold on to the money; it slipped through my fingers like a snake. For instance, I bought a valuable violin, made of silky, sunny wood. I never played it; it was too late. The instrument lay in its coffin-case like an expensive toy. I indulged myself in this old whim, the image of a dream that never came true. I still carry that violin with me wherever I go, from move to move; it follows me like a faithful dog; it has its place of honor in a wardrobe. It won't sing and my childhood has fallen silent with it. He was gifted, that boy; he hid in an attic and scratched away at his violin by candlelight. The dog woke and howled. He had a fortune in his fingers. But not everyone can do what he wants, and there's always life to get in your way, to empty your pockets and your illusions. You don't have the hands for nursing a violin. The instrument is like a beetle's shell, it doesn't hold up under your square fingers. Leave it for other people. Don't dress yourself up with a violin like peacock feathers and try to wake up on time tomorrow to plant potatoes. The reaper's *valse triste*, the *petite suite* for weevils and mildew . . . the music yellowing and cracking, the notes crumbling, faded. No lovelier song in the country than that of our crows and our magpies. The Unfinished Symphony for wind and owl-shit.

FOREIGN BODIES│pp. 67–68.

Cayrol's heroes, like many in the French novel since *The Outsider,* are "pauvres types," who wander about in life dazed, docile, and guileless. Their responses are only the direct and instinctive responses of brutes.

I lived in Bordeaux. It's a city I came to without hopes and which I left without regrets. I decided, "It has to take me to Paris." Bordeaux was a place I already knew. I knew its smell of overripe fruit in summer, its smoke in winter. I didn't know what to do with myself, so I did nothing. The place overpowered me from the start, with its harbor where I shivered in front of the freighters and nibbled the peanuts that fell out of the sacks. I was ready to take on anything, dawdling and suspicious, eating my bread in the shadow of a crane. At night there were good hiding places to sleep in. I had myself a good time without asking anyone for help. I had my favorite hangouts, my habits. I wandered around the same docks at regular hours. I leaned against warehouse walls and I waited.

I wasn't the only one waiting for the day to be over. A woman talked to me, but I was clumsy; she asked me questions I couldn't answer. She led me on, bought me drinks, a ticket to the movies. Finally, in the middle of the film, I went to sleep. When I woke up between features, I was alone. I hadn't said a word to her, but I had followed her docilely enough, playing along with her good humor when she pounded me on the shoulder, patted my arm, looked at me greedily. She had turned up in my life too soon for me. Who could use me then, or recognize my qualities?

FOREIGN BODIES | pp. 28–29.

REFERENCES

Barthes, Roland. "Jean Cayrol et ses romans," *Esprit*, March, 1952, pp. 482–499.

Dort, Bernard. "Jean Cayrol ou l'avènement au roman," *Cahiers du Sud*, 326 (December, 1954), pp. 132–140.

Pingaud, Bernard. "Jean Cayrol et le trésor," *Les Lettres Nouvelles*, November, 1957.

Lynes, Carlos. "Towards Reconciliation: The World of Jean Cayrol," *Yale French Studies*, 24 (Summer, 1959), pp. 62–67.

Pingaud, Bernard. *Ecrivains d'aujourd'hui.*

## SELECTED WORKS

*Les Impudents* (Plon, 1943).

*La Vie tranquille* (Gallimard, 1944).

*Un Barrage contre le Pacifique* (Gallimard, 1950). Translated by Herma Briffault as *The Sea Wall* (Pellegrini and Cudahy, 1953).

*Le Marin de Gibraltar* (Gallimard, 1952). *Les petits chevaux de Tarquinia* (Gallimard, 1953).

*Des Journées entières dans les arbres* (Gallimard, 1954).

*Le Square* (Gallimard, 1955). Translated by Sonia Pitt-Rivers and Irma Morduch as *The Square* (Grove Press, 1960).

*Moderato Cantabile* (Editions de Minuit, 1958). Translated by Richard Seaver (Grove Press, 1960).

*Dix Heures et demie du soir en été* (Gallimard, 1960). Translated by Anne Borchardt as *Ten-thirty on a Summer Night* (Grove Press, 1962).

*L'Après-midi de Monsieur Andesmas* (Gallimard, 1962).

# MARGUERITE DURAS

Born in Indo-China in 1914, Marguerite Duras went to Paris at the age of seventeen. She studied mathematics at the Sorbonne and took a *licence* both in law and political science. Her fame in literature dates from *Un Barrage contre le Pacifique* (*The Sea Wall*), which was made into a film. Mme. Duras has recently taken a great interest in the cinema, composing the scenario and the dialogue for the prize-winning *Hiroshima mon amour*, which has circulated widely in the United States. As the overtones of the movie might suggest, Marguerite Duras' political sympathies are towards the left. She is no longer, however, a Communist Party member.

Without meaning to belittle Duras' originality or power as a writer, I should like to observe that her novels have always illustrated very well the trend of the times. Her first works date from the 1940's, when the impact of the American novel was felt most strongly in France; the inspiration of Faulkner and Caldwell is evident in *The Sea Wall* and even in the earlier work, *La Vie tranquille*. In the 1950's her novels gradually evolve towards the ideal of the new novel, attaining their goal most perfectly in *The Square*. Her most recent fiction shows a trend towards less rigor and formalism without, however, implying anything like a repudiation of new novel principles. Whether on a farm, a yacht, or a beach, the persons Mme. Duras describes play out the entire drama of human existence. They are all seeking something—meaning of life, fulfillment, or happiness—but their will is a fragile bark soon surrendering to the great currents and waves which carry them on according to plans that are not of human making. As in Simon's novels, time goes on, destinies are accomplished, and life is perhaps over before these nameless persons are fully aware of what has been happening. Their reactions have nothing of Promethean grandeur, but are feeble whinings or petty mutual brutalities.

All this is forcefully presented chiefly by means of dialogue. The novels are full of conversation—a bumbling, inexplicit flow of words that through its very incoherence and fortuity reveals the pathos of these starved lives. Chronology, individualized characters, commentary, specificity of any kind are dispensed with to make dialogue carry the burden of the novel. Marguerite Duras, like Nathalie Sarraute and Ivy Compton-Burnett, shows that it can be done.

Anne Desbaresdes, the young wife of a wealthy industrialist, has been profoundly disturbed by the sight of a man clinging tightly to the body of the woman he has just murdered. Every day she goes back to the little café where the crime took place, next door to where her little boy takes his piano lessons. There she meets a man and drinks wine. Gradually sinking into a stupor she mentally re-enacts the crime of passion which has taken place, she and her strange consort miming the roles of its tragic actors. Working almost exclusively with dialogue, Mme. Duras creates an extraordinarily intense atmosphere of sadistic carnality.

There was only one customer left at the bar. The four others in the room were talking intermittently. A couple came in. The patronne served them, and resumed knitting her red sweater, which she had put aside as long as the bar was crowded. She turned down the radio. The tide was running high that night, breaking loudly against the docks, rising above the songs.

"Once he had realized how much she wanted him to do it, I'd like you to tell me why he didn't do it, say, a little later or . . . a little sooner."

"Really, I know very little about it. But I think that he couldn't make up his mind, couldn't decide whether he wanted her alive or dead. He must have decided very late in the game that he preferred her dead. But that's all pure conjecture."

Anne Desbaresdes was lost in thought, her pale face lowered hypocritically.

"She hoped very much that he would do it."

"It seems to me that he must have hoped so just as much as she did. I don't know really."

"As much as she did?"

"Yes. Don't talk any more."

The four men left. The couple was still sitting there in silence. The woman yawned. Chauvin ordered another bottle of wine.

"Would it be impossible if we didn't drink so much?"

"I don't think it would be possible," Anne Desbaresdes murmured.

She gulped down her glass of wine. He let her go on killing herself. Night had completely occupied the town. The lampposts along the docks were lighted. The child was still playing. The last trace of pink had faded from the sky.

"Before I leave," Anne Desbaresdes begged, "if you could tell me I'd like to know a little more. Even if you're not very sure of your facts."

Chauvin went on, in a flat, expressionless voice that she had not heard from him before.

"They lived in an isolated house, I think it was by the sea. It was hot. Before they went there they didn't realize how quickly things would evolve, that after a few days he would keep having to throw her out. It wasn't long before he was forced to drive her away, away from him, from the house. Over and over again."

"It wasn't worth the trouble."

"It must have been difficult to keep from having such thoughts, you get into the habit, like you get into the habit of living. But it's only a habit."

"And she left?"

"She left when and how he wanted her to, although she wanted to stay."

Anne Desbaresdes stared at that unknown man without recognizing him, like a trapped animal.

"Please," she begged.

"Then the time came when he sometimes looked at her and no longer saw her as he had seen her before. She ceased to be beautiful or ugly, young or old, similar to anyone else, even to herself. He was afraid. It was the last vacation. Winter came. You're going back by the Boulevard de la Mer. It will be the eighth night."

The child came in and snuggled for a moment against his mother. He was still humming the Diabelli sonatina. She stroked his hair, which was very close to her face. The man avoided looking at them. Then the child left.

"So the house was isolated," Anne Desbaresdes said slowly. "It was hot, you said. When he told her to leave she always obeyed. She slept under the trees, or in the fields, like . . ."

"Yes," Chauvin said.

"When he called her she came back. And when he told her to go, she left. To obey him like that was her way of hoping. And even when she reached the threshold she waited for him to tell her to come in."

"Yes."

In a daze, Anne Desbaresdes brought her face close to Chauvin's, but he moved back out of reach.

"And it was there, in that house, that she learned what you said she was, perhaps even . . ."

"Yes, a bitch," Chauvin interrupted her again.

Now it was her turn to draw back. He filled her glass and offered it to her.

"I was lying," he said.

She arranged her hair, which was completely disheveled, and wearily trying to restrain her compassion, got hold of herself.

"No," she said.

Chauvin's face looked inhumanly harsh under the neon light, but she could not take her eyes off him. Again the child ran in from the sidewalk.

"It's dark out now," he announced.

He looked out the door and yawned, then turned back to her and stood beside her, humming.

"See how late it is. Quickly, tell me the rest."

"Then the time came when he thought he could no longer touch her except to . . ."

Anne Desbaresdes raised her hands to her bare neck in the opening of her summer dress.

"Except to . . . this. Am I right?"

"Yes. That."

Her hands let go and slipped from her neck.

"I'd like you to leave," Chauvin murmured.

Anne Desbaresdes got up from her chair and stood motionless in the middle of the room. Chauvin remained seated, overwhelmed, no longer aware of her. Unable to resist, the patronne put her knitting aside, and openly watched them both, but they were oblivious of her stare. It was the child who came to the door and took his mother's hand.

"Come on, let's go."

MODERATO CANTABILE | pp. 89–93.

Of the new novelists, Marguerite Duras is the only one whose themes are heavily sexual. In *Moderato Cantabile*, the image of a man kissing the bloody mouth of the woman he has just killed is conjured up repeatedly in orgiastic visions by the heroine. In *Ten-thirty on a Summer Night,* a drama of passion acted out in symbolic and ultimate terms again frames the story of a woman disturbed by erotic cravings so violent as to involve self-degradation and death-wish.

Maria is a young French woman on vacation in Spain with her husband, her little girl, and a woman companion. Because of severe cloudbursts, they stopped in a little town, where they learned of the murder just committed. Maria, like other Duras heroines, drinks. In her befuddled and unhappy mind, images of her husband making love to their companion mingle with those of the faithless young wife and the husband-murderer. That night she discovers the murderer hiding on a roof opposite her balcony and helps him escape before morning. But her exploit was pointless—he kills himself, and the tourists continue their way. Midday they stop to rest. The moment Maria has been waiting for—the consummation of her husband's adultery—is about to arrive. She is sinking into a drunken stupor, the two lovers are frantic with desire. Mme. Duras presents this climactic scene by understatement, using terse, banal dialogue. Yet its very control heightens its emotional quality. One may think, too, that the release and relief which is the theme of the conversation—the cool haven from the heat, the sensual satisfaction in the food, etc.—anticipate the emotional dénouement about to take place.

> Judith discovered she was hungry and said so.
> They felt unexpectedly at ease because of the coolness of the staggered, crowded rooms.
> 'Was it hot,' Maria said at last.
> They were shown to a table that looked out on the pine trees—they could see them through the blinds and discovered, next to the pines, a small olive grove. There was a path between them. Judith was brought some water. Judith drank and drank. They watched her drink. Then she stopped.
> Maria was between Claire and Pierre. Surrounded by them. Even they had ordered a manzanilla. Judith was coming back to life and began to move about between their table and the entrance to the inn.

Maria was drinking manzanillas.

'It's good,' she said. 'I think I'll drink forever.'

She drank. Claire stretched out on the bench and laughed.

'Just as you like, Maria,' she said.

She threw a quick, circular glance of happiness around her. The dining room was full. It was summer, in Spain. There were fruity food smells in the air about that time, every day, and they always made you feel somewhat nauseous.

'I'm not at all hungry,' Claire announced.

'We're not hungry,' Maria said.

Pierre smoked and drank his manzanilla. Ever since their trip had begun, he was silent, for long periods of time, between these two women.

Pierre ordered fried shrimp. Maria asked for good, tender meat for Judith. It was promised. They put Judith on a chair piled with cushions, the only one at the table.

'We could have arranged a good life for him,' Maria began, 'and perhaps I would have loved him.'

'Who will ever know?' Claire said.

They laughed together, then were silent, and then Maria went on drinking manzanillas.

Judith was brought some acceptable meat. Then they brought the fried shrimp and olives.

Judith ate well.

'Finally,' Pierre said, looking at his child, 'finally she's hungry.'

'The storm,' Claire said. 'This morning she was hungry too.'

Judith, well behaved, was eating. Maria was cutting her meat. She chewed and swallowed. Maria cut some more. They ate while watching Judith eat so nicely. The shrimps were fresh and hot, cracking under their teeth, smelling of fire.

'Do you like it, Pierre?' Claire said.

She had one in her mouth. You could hear her teeth biting into it. Again she was unable to escape her desire for Pierre. She had left her ferociousness behind, she was beautiful again, saved from the menace that Rodrigo Paestra had been, alive. Her voice was like honey when she asked him—her voice was completely transformed—whether he liked it, as much as she.

'They'll find him in a while,' Maria said, 'in about four hours. In the meantime, he's still in the wheat field.'

'You know, to talk about it won't change anything,' Claire said.

'I still feel like it,' Maria said. 'Must you stop me?'

'No,' Pierre said, 'no, Maria. Why?'

Maria drank some more. The shrimp were the best in Spain. Maria asked for more. They were eating more than they had thought they would. And, while Maria was giving in to her tiredness, Claire was coming to life like Judith, and devoured the shrimps. The same shrimps he was eating.

'We had hardly started playing, when the game was lost,' Maria went on. 'Lost games like that make you rationalize endlessly.'

'It would have pleased me very much to save Rodrigo Paestra,' Pierre said, 'I must admit.'

'It wasn't the sun, was it?' Claire asked.

'It was the sun,' Pierre said.

Judith was no longer hungry. She was willing to have an orange. Pierre peeled it for her with great care. Judith followed this with envious attention.

They were no longer hungry.

TEN-THIRTY ON A SUMMER NIGHT | pp. 85–88.

REFERENCES

Mauriac, Claude. "L'étouffant univers de Marguerite Duras," *Le Figaro Littéraire*, March 12, 1958.

Picon, Gaëtan. "Les romans de Marguerite Duras," *Mercure de France*, June, 1958, pp. 309–314.

Luccioni, Gennie. "Marguerite Duras et le roman abstrait," *Esprit*, July–August, 1958, pp. 73–76.

Blanchot, Maurice. *Le Livre à venir.*

Hoog, Armand. "The Itinerary of Marguerite Duras," *Yale French Studies*, 24 (Summer, 1959), pp. 68–73.

Pingaud, Bernard. *Ecrivains d'aujourd'hui.*

## SELECTED WORKS

*Le Pire* (Gallimard, 1954).

*Les Vainqueurs du Jaloux* (Gallimard, 1957).

# JEAN LAGROLET

Jean Lagrolet was born in Bayonne in 1918. Having lost his mother at birth, he was brought up by relatives, who sent him first to a religious school, then to the university to study law and political science. He was a prisoner during the war. Having a private income, Lagrolet has not applied himself to any calling or profession. To date, he has written two volumes, the second of which has associated him with the new novel.

*Le Pire* is a brief myth depicting a little kingdom whose sovereign, on his deathbed, reveals to his people that God does not exist and that his own power to rule rested upon nothing. As the now liberated subjects go on quarreling over the patrimony as if it had a price, the new king watches with indifference and decides to rule wholly arbitrarily. The author goes on to argue the wisdom of arbitrary acts.

*Les Vainqueurs du Jaloux* is the story of a man who resides in the country and works for a celebrated architect. By contrast with Lagrolet's first work, this is a real novel—in appearance a conventional novel of analysis told in the first person. On closer inspection, however, we realize that this novel is only in appearance conventional, that it is really a sort of anti-novel, not to be taken at face value. We suspect that Gilles, the narrator, is a liar, that he is frequently the opposite of what he makes himself out to be. The author never really lets us know about Gilles or about any of the other characters, who remain enigmatic and full of contradictions, not only as to their real nature but as to their mutual relations.

The central scene in *Les Vainqueurs du Jaloux* is a luncheon given by Gilles' neighbor, Robert Sens, in honor of his son, Antoine, who has come to visit him in his country house,

Glains. Besides the narrator and his companion, Françoise, the guests include Barbara and Jean-Francis, the children of the architect Benoît Freyburger and eventually Freyburger himself. The dialogue, extracts of which are translated below, should be compared with usual dialogue simulating real conversation. Instead of the conventional talk of the realistic novel, in which characters either hide their real feelings by what they say or make significant remarks designed by the author to further his story, here the characters alternate between obvious play-acting and spontaneous outbursts. We have the impression of listening to a company of frenzied neurotics, and are reminded of some of Dostoievsky's dialogue. There are points in common, too, between this babble and the conversation of Ivy Compton-Burnett and Nathalie Sarraute. The host, Robert, has come in from the garden to find Gilles and Françoise talking to Antoine. Robert's wife, Annette, also appears. The Freyburger children are late. Here is some of the conversation, lifted from the descriptions, explanations, and commentaries in which it is embedded:

"Since we are obliged to wait for them, let's have a drink to pass the time," said Robert.

"You ought not to drink alcohol," Antoine observed, shaking his head. "It is not good for you."

"Your son is right," Annette said, appearing in the door. "You ruin your health for nothing. My boy, I have tried to fix as good a dinner as possible in your honor, unfortunately we have had only Madeleine to help us, and she isn't much of a cook. I have had to tell her everything to do and to lend a hand myself. Anyway, pot luck, it seems to me that what's nice about it is to be together as a family and to be surrounded by real friends."

"I didn't come to have a good dinner but to see Papa and you."

"The one does not prevent the other," Annette said.

"Let's have a drink," Robert said, serving us some absinth.

---

"How impossible and rude those young Freyburgers are," Robert said.

And Annette,

"Well, there you are, you always act before you think, you invite them and now you have to wait for them, the chicken will be over-cooked."

―――――――

"If they aren't here in five minutes, we are going to start to eat," said Robert. "I don't know what got into me to invite them. Pity, doubt-less, for they are of absolutely no interest. But you don't realize, Antoine, what a splendid fellow Gilles is, the finest this locality produces, and you'd be really surprised how remarkable he is."

"I assure you that I do not doubt it," said Antoine in a perfectly indifferent voice.

―――――――

Annette and Françoise had begun to chat out on the porch while drinking a strawberryade. Suddenly Robert jumped up, quite red in the face and brandishing an empty glass, "I don't want us to wait for them any longer. I am the master in my own house."

Antoine looked at him curiously, gave a little laugh, "Let's not wait since you get on edge about it and rudeness still amuses you. But I don't see why we are in such a hurry, I have plenty of time today."

"What I do is never rude," Robert said. "Everybody at Glains should do what I want."

His impatience drove him to baring his most secret thoughts and even his puerile notion of happiness. He glanced at us to demand our approbation, but only Antoine saw fit to declare,

"After all, as you please. You are perhaps right. But it seems to me that one cannot treat in such a cavalier fashion the children of an im-portant person like M. Freyburger."

"M. Freyburger is important only in his own eyes."

―――――――

As we were about to sit down, at his request, Jean-Francis ap-peared in the doorway. I thought for an instant that his sister wouldn't come, but she was ten yards behind him, and I could see the cross ex-pression on her face through the window.

―――――――

"Well, here you are at last!" cried Robert to our two neighbors, "we weren't waiting for you any longer. You are people who have no sense of time, and one must always act as if such people did not exist. That is what puts you at ease, I suppose?"

"You know, Sir, it's not my fault," stammered Jean-Francis, looking at his sister, who was shrugging her shoulders. The frightful green and red tie which was strangling him assumed more importance than his face.

"I imagined as much," Robert replied, seizing him by the arm, as he usually did me to my great displeasure.

Antoine was standing before the fireplace, rolling the stem of a glass of absinth with his finger tips. He suddenly went over to Jean-Francis, whom his father had just released.

"You can gulp this down before going to table," he said, "it is good contraband, I haven't touched it, and there is nothing more refreshing. I don't at all understand why my father is in a hurry today, I never understand why he is in a hurry. He is a man who has nothing to do. And it is not so late . . ."

"What makes me in a hurry, my children, why, it's joy! One must give in to it. Let's eat right away."

I knew very well that Antoine had drunk from his glass before offering it to Jean-Francis, and I admired his presence of mind, his way of saving the vulgar situation in which Robert, who had not bothered to give them a drink, placed us all *vis-à-vis* the Freyburgers . . .

————

I then whispered in his ear . . . , "You know that you astound me. There is nothing I admire so much as the knack of knowing the suitable thing to do—something I myself do not possess—and I was well aware just now that you had drunk from your glass before giving it to Jean-Francis, so that he would not feel offended."

Then an inhuman anger swept over his face.

"You are a perfect fool," he said.

LES VAINQUEURS DU JALOUX|pp. 124–132.

REFERENCES

Arland, Marcel. "Plaisirs et tourments de l'ambiguïté," *La Nouvelle Revue Française,* January, 1957, pp. 122–127.

Vriguy, Roger. "L'Ecrivain à la recherche d'une méthode," *La Parisienne,* March, 1957, pp. 374–378.

Pingaud, Bernard. *Ecrivains d'aujourd'hui.*

SELECTED WORKS


*La Mise en scène* (Editions de Minuit, 1958).


*Le Maintien de l'ordre* (Gallimard, 1961).

# CLAUDE OLLIER

Claude Ollier was born in 1922 in Paris. After his studies, which culminated in a *licence* in law, he worked five years for the government in Morocco. He has travelled widely in Europe, North Africa, North and Central America. In 1959 he visited the United States on a grant for young artists, obtained on the strength of his first novel, published the year before. *La Mise en scène* was followed in 1961 by *Le Maintien de l'ordre*. Ollier is a disciple of Robbe-Grillet, and his two novels adhere quite closely to the formula of the new novel, particularly in their emphasis upon "objectal" description.

*La Mise en scène* is the account of an engineer sent to map out a road in the mountainous hinterland of North Africa. He finds himself in a strange hallucinatory world, pursuing a quest he knows doomed to failure. On his path he discovers traces of another European there before him, whose story he suspects of being tragic and violent but which he never succeeds in piecing together. The procedures typical of the new novel are here in full evidence, with descriptions à la Robbe-Grillet and a plot that strongly recalls *Passing Time*.

Note in the following how the illusion of a scene observed is created by strict limitation to the single viewer: the author of a new novel, in principle at least, is restricted to what one person can see or know. What is hidden can only be conjectured.

The green eyes, attentive, unusually far apart, seem placed on the edge of the temples, beyond the rise of the cheekbones. The forehead is wide and high, the lower part of the face very narrow. The foreward tilt of the head shows up two concentric curves: the line of the brows and that of the pliant, delicate lips. The very black hair is separated by a center part and dressed in braids which go around the ears and fall on the front of the shoulders.

The arms thrown back give the breast a firmer and clearer outline. The right hand is clutching, behind the nape of the neck, the upper edge of a handle; the left one disappears, on a level with the hip, towards the bottom of the water jug or the lower edge of the other handle. The jug—a sort of amphora with a long cylindrical neck—rests all its weight on the lower back. The red and white striped dress is caught about the waist by a very wide band of material in which gold and black checks alternate. The neck is adorned with a necklace of silver pieces strung on a silk cord. Metal bracelets slip from the wrist towards the elbow, along the right forearm. The left wrist is hidden by the nape of the neck.[1]

The silhouette is outlined against the lusterless light of the sky. The girl has stopped in the middle of the field, half-way between the tree and the dry stone wall. The bust is bent forward, the head slightly turned: the glance seems to plunge obliquely towards the object which it has happened upon, a few meters from there: the stranger lying under the walnut tree, his head propped up and leaning partially on the trunk of the tree, partially on a cardboard portfolio standing vertical against the bark; one hand supports the nape of the neck, the other holds a piece of wood— a pencil or the stem of a pipe—placed right on the ground among the bits of straw and the sheets of paper.

Lassalle had just opened his eyes. Perhaps they had been half-open for several instants, for she has fled . . . She was in front of him, three or four meters from the tree, in the very middle of the field, and now she is running away, she glides with smooth easy little steps along the furrow parallel to the wall.

LA MISE EN SCÈNE | p. 82.

Elaborately composed tableaux are a feature of the new art of Robbe-Grillet, Claude Simon, and Claude Ollier. They may be symbolic, not in a precise or specifically translatable way, but in the sense that they reinforce the theme or heighten the atmosphere. The dread and fear of the European wanderer through the vast desert, who senses himself surrounded and menaced by the invisible forces of untamed nature, are projected in the following image of horror and revulsion:

[1] Apparently there is some error here, for it is difficult to imagine how the left wrist could be hidden by the nape of the neck.

There are surely two hundred of them, black, very tiny, working away at top speed, concentrated on an exceptional task worthy of mobilizing all their energies.

They have already devoured a good half of the animal, beginning at the sting and the curling extremity of the tail. They are now attacking the last portions of the abdomen, the nippers, the head, the legs still curved in position for locomotion.

The scorpion's carcass seems enormous. The tiny black points slip on the rough carapace, as if they could not master it, and yet get through it, crack it, pierce it, empty it of its content, suck it, digest it and work over the remnants which imperceptibly get smaller, flake off, blow away.

It was probably a black scorpion, of modest size, of the most widespread species in the region, small, very venomous. But it is gray at present, sand-colored, dirty, almost colorless . . . Deprived of its weapon, amputated everywhere, reduced to a few linear elements of tough matter, to a few transparent plane surfaces, it reminds one of an old, useless celluloid toy.

The dismembering goes on minutely. The horny substance comes apart bit by bit, immediately swallowed. There are too many ants: many of them crawl up the legs, jostle and climb over one another, fall on their backs, turn themselves over and go at it again. Some, incapable of getting to the booty and having their share, give up, move to one side and watch helplessly the remainder of the feast.

The eight curved legs are in position for locomotion, ready to resume their travels, as if the catastrophe had caught them in full motion, and the whole animal, still adhering to the rock by the abdomen and the extremities of the legs, seems to have passed without transition from joyous vigor to annihilation.

The rock is in the shadow. The whole field is in the shadow, all the bottom of the valley: the sun has not yet reached the granary roof. Opposite, the line of the shadow slowly descends across the plateau: in a few instants it will touch the top of the hill of red soil.

LA MISE EN SCÈNE | pp. 205–206.


Like Michel Butor's *Passing Time*, Ollier's novel is a detective story without an ending. The hero puzzles over the drawings he has copied in his notebook from some stones observed during his mapping expedition. They are clues among many others to the drama that he suspects to have occurred in the region. But they lead him nowhere, no further than the bits of conversation overheard, the inconsistent and evasive answers to his questions. His failure is the same as that of Butor's hero, who despite a multiplicity of signs, can never thread his way back to what actually did take place, if anything.

Farther off, on the last pages of the notebook, figure the pencil drawings, awkward but precise, copied from the flat stones of tizi n'Oualoun—club, spear, cog-wheel, sun—and on the following page, the complete reproduction of the carvings on the ogival stone: the man on horseback brandishing the mallet, the child crouching before him, and on the other side of the body stretched out, arms crossed, lying on the ground or buried upright in the soil, finally the second animal, with hoof raised, that is turning away or making off . . . The man has just been struck, his mount is abandoning him; the horseman at present turns towards the child and is preparing to inflict upon it the same fate. . . . But that would be postulating a double murder and lending it all sorts of motives: rite, vengeance, betrayal, jealousy . . . Nothing evidently prevents considering the five figures as a single tableau: many relationships arise out of simple juxtaposition, even when no such groupings were part of the original notion.

LA MISE EN SCÈNE|p. 199.

In *Le Maintien de l'ordre* the setting is likewise North Africa, but, instead of the desert wastes of *La Mise en scène*, we have here a large city with its modern quarters and its old native district. The narrator, presumably a government worker, is being shadowed by a pair of gunmen. Fragmentary scenes and dialogues suggest a story taking place during the early years of the Algerian troubles, a story involving "pacification" problems and an unfortunate case of recourse to collusion with a gang. Ollier's novel is in no sense a pamphlet, however—the situation serves only to portray the sentiments of a tracked man, whose instinct of self-protection weakens through this monotonous and implacable surveillance, revives fitfully at moments of alarm, but ultimately seems to dissolve in indecision and lassitude. The work is structured on the narrator's oscillating moods and is without an ending. Reiterated reference to the heat of the city, to the mist that shrouds the harbor in the morning—in fact all the "objectal" word-painting that fills the pages—serves to produce a sort of pathetic fallacy. The maze of streets through which the narrator drives his Fiat suggests the tangled predicament in which the hero finds himself. No precise explanation of the predicament is given however. The reader is asked to live the narrator's actual experience—see what he sees at a given moment, feel what he feels.

As the novel opens, the narrator must be posted at his window. His gaze covers the scene like a movie camera, first with panoramic "shots," then with "close-ups."

On a great screen uniform and smooth, stretched from one end of the horizon to the other, glistens a pale, fine dust, a grayish haze veiling the vibrations of the air and the eddies of the water. High above, rolling in from the open sea, big clouds pile up, break apart, and slowly go off towards the north; below, long waves break on the shoals and spread over the flat rocks edging the shore. In the space between, the transition takes place imperceptibly; sky and sea are melted in a blurred, translucent substance the color of lead. No dividing line intervenes: at every point the same filtered light shines through with a bright and blinding glare.

Farther down, inscribed in a frame less vast, countless straight lines make up a network of unequal quadrilaterals, joined at right angles to each other like the blocks of a scale model, certain ones placed vertically—façades of large new apartments on the water front, fences, red earth walls around the old city—, most of them piled up horizontally, without apparent order—tops of sheds, warehouse covers, flat roofs of the native houses, separated by little whitewashed walls. Laundry is drying on these roofs: hundreds of bits of fabric flap in the wind.

Closer by lies the square of greenery of Wilson Park. Two wide diagonal paths intersect at a circle dominated by a statue. The circle is surrounded by stretches of dry grass bordered by araucarias and palm trees whose drab, bluish leaves are for the moment perfectly still. On the perimeter of the park, two rows of eucalyptus trees make parallel lines: the low branches are scarcely moving, only the high foliage stirs.

Still closer, as though leaned against the trees, are spaced out the components of the bowling club, squeezed between the park and the avenue: to the left, the covered buildings—refreshment stand, dressing rooms, restaurant—, to the right, the bowling lanes—eight rectangles of ochre earth separated by little wooden fences. The players haven't arrived yet. A young boy, barefoot, is manipulating the nozzle of a hose, behind which trails a long black rubber tube. He brandishes the nozzle obliquely towards the sky: the water sparkles and falls back down as rain.

Very near, but invisible, way down on the avenue, a bus goes by, its horn sounding hoarse. The noise of the motor and the vibrations from the thoroughfare reverberate all over the building, from the entry with its wrought-iron pillars to the windows on the top floor.

The panes of the wide-open casement window vibrate, then the thin walls of the bedroom, the bedroom door, and on the other side, two steps out on the landing, the door of the elevator shaft, which, being heavier, reverberates longer, with a more hollow sound. But maybe it would reverberate anyway, without the noise of the bus . . . Maybe it's still reverberating from that sudden slam just a few seconds ago, from that brutal, hasty closing just before the bursting into the room and the less resonant, almost echoless slam of the bedroom door—fragile rampart, first resting spot, facing the wide-open window, first pause, time for a brief respite, the few moments necessary to catch one's breath.

The elevator door keeps on reverberating: it's as though its iron handle were still vibrating in the palm of a hand.

The bus goes on its way: the vibrations grow fainter. Several cars follow in its wake, leaving no other trace than a clear, light hum punctuated by two very short toots of a horn. After this no more vehicles pass by on the avenue . . . The window panes have stopped vibrating, and so have the walls of the bedroom, and the door. Everything seems calm also on the other side of the door. The elevator hasn't started up again; the car must still be at the floor, there where it came to a stop one minute before. And no one has had time yet to come up the stairs as far as the eighth.

Nothing indicates, moreover, that anybody at all is coming up the stairs or at least approaching the top floors. No noise filters through the wooden panel: no measured tread, no furtive scraping on the imitation marble of the steps, nor the bump of the toe of a shoe against the balusters . . . All is still. If someone is coming up at this moment, it can only be in the lower part of the staircase.

Just the same, better make sure, for whatever it's worth, since there's still time . . . There's still time to open the door again and go glance at the landing.

The knob clicks in the lock, the bolt comes out of the catch, the door turns slowly on its hinges: in the narrow opening, the first steps of the staircase are coming into sight, then the balusters, and a little more to the left, behind the staircase, the grilled shaft which, having emerged from the depths of the building, rises still a few more yards up to the roof which it seems to pierce through with its metallic rods.

LE MAINTIEN DE L'ORDRE|pp. 9–13.

## REFERENCES

Rousseaux, André. "Un disciple de Robbe-Grillet," *Le Figaro Littéraire,* November 8, 1958.

Ms., P. "Les Médicis (nouveau jury) débutent . . . en couronnant *La Mise en scène,*" *Le Figaro Littéraire,* November 29, 1958.

Howlett, Jacques. "La Mise en scène," *Les Lettres Nouvelles,* January, 1959, pp. 122–125.

Albérès, René M. "Le Monde des Livres," *Les Nouvelles Littéraires,* August 17, 1961.

Ricardou, Jean. "Aventures et Mésaventures de la description," *Critique,* November, 1961, pp. 937–949.

SELECTED WORKS

*Entre Fantoine et Agapa* (Laffont, 1950).

*Mahu ou le Matériau* (Laffont, 1952). Republished by Editions de Minuit, 1957.

*Graal Flibuste* (Editions de Minuit, 1956).

*Baga* (Editions de Minuit, 1958).

*Le Fiston* (Editions de Minuit, 1958). Translated by Richard Howard as *Monsieur Levert* (Grove Press, 1961).

*Clope au dossier* (Editions de Minuit, 1961).

# ROBERT PINGET

Born in Geneva in 1920, Robert Pinget did his secondary studies in classics, then took a degree in law and passed his bar examinations. He has also studied painting. Familiar with England, where he taught for a year, he has travelled extensively throughout Europe and North Africa too. In 1960 Pinget received a Ford Foundation grant under which he visited for six months in the United States.

Pinget exhibited in his first works a gratuitous fantasy taking the form of comic parodies and allegories. One finds everything from Ubuesque inventions to shaggy dog stories, the sort of thing that would delight critics bent on liquidating the conventional novel. They have jubilantly hailed Pinget as one who has turned the old novel inside out, destroyed its characters, language, and plot. However that may be, in 1958, with *Le Fiston* (*Monsieur Levert*), Pinget definitely joined the ranks of the new novelists. Leaving off his loony antics, he tells the story of a man working every night on a letter to his son. We soon lose all foothold in reality as we enter the troubled universe of this father whose son has gone away. When did he actually leave, when is he coming back, will he ever return? We cannot trust the father's account, for it is obviously all mixed up, yet it is our only source of information. We try to infer what the facts of the story are but our view is so hampered by the obscurity and confusion of his vision that we give up and just listen with hypnotized attention.

During the season of 1959–1960, at the Salle Récamier, Pinget presented an adaptation of *Monsieur Levert* for the theater, which he called *Lettre morte*. Inversely, of his burlesque piece *La Manivelle*, which Beckett translated for the English radio, Pinget made a nondramatic version entitled *Clope au dossier* (1961). In *Monsieur Levert*, a father tried to put into a letter the goings-on in his town; in *Clope*, a madman assembles a dossier for his defense and incorporates in it a whole chronicle of a little town. In both works we hear a constant prattle—clichés, argot, banal conversation, mumblings and ravings. Through it our ear catches the authentic ring of the rural French community, the author's merciless satire, and the pathos of tragic existences.

Pinget's collaboration with Samuel Beckett is an interesting development in his career. In 1957 he had translated *All That Fall* of the Franco-Irish playwright.

Monsieur Levert is here giving an account of the death of a local girl, the cobbler's daughter, who may have wasted away, pining for a young man who had, some years before, spent his vacation with the family. He begins forthrightly enough, but soon wanders off into a maze of musings and recollections from which he comes out at the beginning again. Each time the story is told it is altered—facts are modified in themselves and in their significance; characters change, swap their stories, even their age and their name. But the father writes doggedly on, becoming more and more muddled as he goes on, even lapsing into gibberish.

Pinget's work joins the others, particularly Butor's and Ollier's, as the account of a futile attempt to capture reality and make sense of experience.

The shoemaker's daughter is dead. The funeral was last Thursday. The family was there, and a few other people. Madame Chinze, the mother, was so wrapped up in black crepe you couldn't see her at all, which was just as well. Old Chinze had on his black suit and carried a derby. He's shorter than his wife, bald with thick eyebrows. Their older boy, Roger, had driven over from Le Rouget with his pregnant wife and some friends. He looked pale, he has kidney trouble.

———————  pp. 7–8.

I'm trying to remember. Twenty years since I've been there and still. In this place, the old shivers the same fear of what's to come. I haven't learned a thing. I'm going on. The shoemaker's daughter is dead, I went back to the bar. Mochaz and Simonot were there. Not so loud. You know Mochaz, he's related to the Moules, he married one of their cousins.

His wife is one of their cousins. He works because of their little boy Cyrille or Myrtil, he drank a lot. Meanwhile Simonot was talking to Olga. Mochaz told me about his little boy and I talked about mine, son. His house overlooks the Good Sisters' garden, his wife wants to move. Simonot told us about his wife or the opposite. And little by little our childhoods. I had another beer. He's all right except for having to put everything in the plural. Woman, drinks, money. A bachelor's habit, he said. It's a disease of the times. She doesn't have enough to pay her gas any more, doesn't want to get up any more, doesn't want anything except that. She buttoned up his fly for him. Bad day. Talked about this and that, boring as she is, her red nails tapping the zinc counter, old woman's hands, that's what you have. I moved back. The stool fell over and broke . . .

---

My son, I said, you've seen him, he was really fond of you he'll come back don't worry. It was raining outside. People wanted to come in. Their luggage piled up on the sidewalk, not a penny in their pockets, old worn-out shoes. Knock knock. Don't come in. In the name of Christian principles. My poor old father, my poor old mother, old sister, old brother, etc. The door still doesn't open. They force it open . . .

---

. . . someone comes over, I've seen you somewhere, it was in the cemetery I think. I'm not sure because you left right away. A relative of the Chinzes or the Narres or God knows who on a so-called mortuary path. How many pills or poisons mixed up in that story, unworthy mother, old skinflint, house-keeper, country house, ten years of shame, illegitimate son or daughter, leaving, drinking, bar, spoiled spring, terraces with a low wall, gravel crunching at night, letters, letters. I heard the sparrow cheeping on the arbor. Gray day. No one at the windows. The hearse came back empty. To the kingdom of the dead. Rubbed out. Blind men and kings. To the kingdom of the blind where the dead are kings.[1] One-eyed men. Confusion of the blind on this path where so-called funereal where so-called funereal the shoemaker's daughter the maker's. Blind. The maker's. The doeshaughter's baker is mead. The thurlyal few stal worsly. The chanzily wether and a fur pafel. Chadam inze smother wasso repticlap bake beavertall. Westicell. Cold chazzon. Sack boot darryda barry. Seesawter wins thef. Bald ithikye. Gerol verdinover gerol. Nepger few. Pooked lape tridal bikney. Ma. Spine by letter. By imagine. Will leave at daylight.

[1] Confusion of the proverb: In the country of the blind, the one-eyed man is king.

MONSIEUR LEVERT|pp. 62–64.

REFERENCES

Pingaud, Bernard. "Le Fiston," *Les Lettres Nouvelles,* March 4, 1959, pp. 14–15.

Parros, Georges. "Le Fiston," *La Nouvelle Revue Française,* May, 1959, pp. 915–917.

Ollier, Claude. "Le Fiston," *La Nouvelle Revue Française,* September, 1959, pp. 532–534.

Pingaud, Bernard. *Ecrivains d'aujourd'hui.*

SELECTED WORKS

*Les Gommes* (Editions de Minuit, 1953). Translated by Richard Howard as *The Erasers* (Grove Press, 1962).

*Le Voyeur* (Editions de Minuit, 1955). Translated by Richard Howard as *The Voyeur* (Grove Press, 1958).

*La Jalousie* (Editions de Minuit, 1957). Translated by Richard Howard as *Jealousy* (Grove Press, 1959).

*Dans le Labyrinthe* (Editions de Minuit, 1959). Translated by Richard Howard as *In the Labyrinth* (Grove Press, 1960).

*Instantanés* (Editions de Minuit, 1962).

"Une Voie pour le roman futur," *La Nouvelle Revue Française,* July, 1956, pp. 77–84. Translated by Richard Howard as "A Fresh Start for Fiction," *Evergreen Review,* I, 3 (1957), 97–104.

"L'Avenir du roman," *Critique,* August–September, 1956, pp. 697–701.

"Nature, humanisme, tragédie," *La Nouvelle Revue Française,* October, 1958, pp. 580–604. Translated by Bruce Morrissette as "Old 'Values' and the New Novel," *Evergreen Review,* III, 9 (1959), 98–118.

"Le 'nouveau roman,'" *La Revue de Paris,* September, 1961, pp. 115–121.

# ALAIN
# ROBBE-GRILLET

Born August 18, 1922, in Brest, Alain Robbe-Grillet took his secondary schooling in Paris and subsequently studied at the Institut National Agronomique. He worked for a time in the Institut National de Statistique and in the Institut des Fruits et Agrumes coloniaux, his research and assignments sending him to Morocco, Equatorial Africa, and to the French Antilles. At present he holds an executive position in the publishing company, Les Editions de Minuit.

It is around the person of this brilliant and aggressive young writer that most of the hubbub over the new novel has turned. *Les Gommes* aroused sympathetic curiosity, on the whole, and won for Robbe-Grillet a Boswell in Roland Barthes. Hostility towards Robbe-Grillet on the part of established critics stems largely from his polemics, beginning with an article in the *Nouvelle Revue Française* of July, 1956, which dismissed the French novel as being futile and lagging dreadfully behind the times. François Mauriac promptly administered a slap to the young upstart in the *Figaro Littéraire*, and reactions from all quarters were soon forthcoming.[1] *Le Voyeur* brought Robbe-Grillet to the frontiers of the wide public, but the opinion of the experts was still undecided. He gained new supporters and lost old ones. *La Jalousie* likewise met with divergent reactions, even among the younger, less conservative critics. Claude Mauriac declared that with this book Robbe-Grillet had finally produced an excellent novel and an authentic one.[2] On the other hand, Bernard Dort withdrew his support after reading *La Jalousie*, declaring that if Robbe-Grillet had done away with psychology, this book showed

[1] See Introduction, p. 2.
[2] *L'Alittérature Contemporaine*, p. 239.

that he had created ever so bad a myth.[3] For François Erval, *Dans le Labyrinthe* is Robbe-Grillet's most successful work to date, but, as such, it exposes the limitations of "objectal" writing.[4] The case of Robbe-Grillet has not yet been settled. But even the critics he annoys most with his theories and contentions recognize in him a writer of remarkable gifts. The question they cannot answer is whether these gifts may not be wasted in pursuing a chimerical literary objective.

Robbe-Grillet's minute attention to objective details has been the point of departure for all discussions of the new fictional techniques. Its philosophical and esthetic implications have been commented upon heatedly and at length by critics and the author himself. Much about it that seems strange or fortuitous—and, we may say as well, vastly significant—disappears when we interpret a passage like the following as the subjective vision of a single observer of the scene. Mathias is on the ferryboat making ready to dock at the island. What we have before us is the scene as reflected in Mathias' consciousness, a "phenomenological" description of the pier.

The pier, now quite close, towered several yards above the deck. The tide must have been out. The landing slip from which the ship would be boarded revealed the smoother surface of its lower section, darkened by the water and half-covered with greenish moss. On closer inspection, the stone rim drew almost imperceptibly closer.

The stone rim—an oblique, sharp edge formed by two intersecting perpendicular planes: the vertical embankment perpendicular to the quay and the ramp leading to the top of the pier—was continued along its upper side at the top of the pier by a horizontal line extending straight toward the quay.

The pier, which seemed longer than it actually was as an effect of perspective, extended from both sides of this base line in a cluster of parallels describing, with a precision accentuated even more sharply by the morning light, a series of elongated planes alternately horizontal and vertical: the crest of the massive parapet that protected the tidal basin

[3] "Sur les romans de Robbe-Grillet," *Les Temps Modernes*, June, 1957, pp. 1989–1999.
[4] "Dans le Labyrinthe," *Express*, October 1, 1959.

from the open sea, the inner wall of the parapet, the jetty along the top of the pier, and the vertical embankment that plunged straight into the water of the harbor. The two vertical surfaces were in shadow, the other two brilliantly lit by the sun—the whole breadth of the parapet and all of the jetty save for one dark narrow strip: the shadow cast by the parapet. Theoretically, the reversed image of the entire group could be seen reflected in the harbor water, and, on the surface, still within the same play of parallels, the shadow cast by the vertical embankment extending straight toward the quay.

At the end of the jetty the structure grew more elaborate; the pier divided into two parts: on the parapet side, a narrow passageway leading to a beacon light, and on the left the landing slip sloping down into the water. It was this latter inclined rectangle, seen obliquely, that attracted notice; slashed diagonally by the shadow of the embankment it skirted, it showed up as one dark triangle and one bright. All other surfaces were blurred. The water in the harbor was not calm enough for the reflection of the pier to be distinguished. Similarly the shadow of the pier appeared only as a vague strip constantly broken by surface undulations. The shadow of the parapet on the jetty tended to blend into the vertical surface which cast it. Jetty and parapet alike were still encumbered with drying fish, empty crates, large wicker baskets—crayfish and lobster traps, oyster hampers, crab snares. The crowd gathered for the ship's arrival circulated with some difficulty among the various piles of objects.

The ship itself floated so low on the ebb tide that it became impossible to see anything from its deck save the vertical embankment extending straight toward the quay and interrupted at its other end, just in front of the beacon, by the oblique landing slip—its lower section smoother, darkened by the water, and half-covered with greenish moss—still the same distance from the deck, as if all movement were at an end.

Nevertheless, on closer inspection the stone rim drew almost imperceptibly nearer.

The morning sun, slightly overcast as usual, indicated shadows faintly, yet sufficiently to divide the slope into two symmetrical parts, one darker, one brighter, slanting a sharp point of light toward the bottom where the water rose along the slope, lapping between the strands of seaweed.

The movement bringing the little steamer nearer the triangle of stone that thus emerged from the darkness was itself an oblique one, and so deliberate as to be constantly approaching absolute immobility.

Measured and even, despite slight variations of amplitude and rhythm perceptible to the eye but scarcely exceeding six inches and two or three seconds, the sea rose and fell in the sheltered angle formed by the landing slip. On the lower section of this inclined plane the water alternately revealed and submerged great clumps of green seaweed. From time to time, at what were doubtless regular intervals—though probably of a more complex frequency—a powerful wash of water broke this rocking rhythm and the two masses of liquid, rushing against each other, collided with a slapping sound and spattered some drops of foam a little higher up against the embankment.

THE VOYEUR | pp. 6–8.

Robbe-Grillet's unorthodox narrative structure, his violation of chronology, and his repetition (with variation) of anecdote, are apt to disconcert the reader expecting a story forthrightly told. It makes sense, however, if we think of the protagonist's consciousness as being the field of the narrative. There events that are taking place mingle with those which already have taken place, which will take place, or might take place. Memory and imagination function as importantly as immediate perception, and reality is spread over the three. Such a technique sets the mind of the protagonist directly before the reader, revealing it more dramatically than author explanation or other conventional means. At the point in the story where we take the following passage Mathias may have killed the girl after binding her to a tree beside the cliff. The scene in the café is pictured in a muddled and guilty mind.

It was no different now from anywhere else. There was a grocery and a café, of course, almost at the beginning of the village. Leaving his bicycle near the door, Mathias went in.

The arrangement inside was like that of all such establishments in the country or even in the suburbs of big cities—or on the quays of little fishing ports. The girl behind the bar had a timorous face and the ill-assured manners of a dog that had been ill-assured manners of a dog that had been ill-assured manners of a girl who served behind the . . . Behind the bar, a fat woman with a satisfied, jovial face beneath her abundant gray hair was pouring drinks for two workmen in blue overalls. She handled the bottle with the sure gestures of a professional, raising the neck with a slight rotation of her wrist at the precise moment the liquid reached the edge of the glass. The salesman went to the bar, set his suitcase on the floor between his feet, and ordered an absinthe.

Without thinking, the salesman was about to order an absinthe when he changed his mind—just before having spoken the word. He cast about for the name of some other kind of drink, and, unable to think of any, pointed to the bottle the proprietress was still holding after having served the two lighthouse workers.

"I'll have the same," he said, and set the suitcase on the floor between his feet.

The woman put in front of him a glass like the first two; she filled it with her other hand, which had not yet released the bottle—making the same rapid movement, so that a large quantity of liquid was still in the air, between the bottom of the glass and the neck of the bottle, as she was already lifting the latter away. At the very second she had finished twisting her wrist, the surface of the poured liquid immobilized on a level with the edge of the glass—without the slightest meniscus—like a diagram representing the theoretical capacity of the glass.

Its color—rather dark reddish-brown—was that of the majority of wine-base apéritifs. Promptly returned to its place on the shelf, the bottle could not be distinguished from its neighbors in the row of different brands. Previously, when the woman had been holding it in her huge hand, the spread of the fingers—or else the position of the label in relation to the observer—had prevented him from determining its brand. Mathias wanted to reconstruct the scene in order to try to fasten on some fragment of bright-colored paper to compare with the labels lined up on the shelf. He succeeded only in discovering an anomaly which had not struck him at the time: the proprietress used her left hand to serve drinks.

He studied her more attentively as she rinsed and dried the glasses—with the same dexterity—but he could not establish a preliminary standard as to the respective functions of each hand in these complex operations; so that it was impossible for him to determine whether or not she was right- or left-handed. His mind grew so confused between what he saw with his own eyes and his recollection of the previous scene that he began to muddle right and left himself.

The woman put down her towel; she seized the coffee mill beside her, sat down on a stool, and began to turn the handle vigorously. In order not to tire either arm at such a speed, she ground the coffee with one arm and then the other alternately.

The coffee beans made a pattering noise as they were crushed in the gearing, and when one of the two men said something to his companion Mathias could not hear him clearly. Several syllables, however, took shape in his mind, resembling the word "cliff" and—less positively— the verb "to bind." He cocked his ears; but no one was speaking any longer.

The salesman found it strange that they had fallen silent in this way ever since he had come in, sipping their apéritifs and putting their glasses on the bar after each swallow. Perhaps he had disturbed them in the midst of an important conversation. He tried to imagine what it could be about. But suddenly he was afraid to guess, and dreaded the possibility that the subject might be broached again, as if their words, without their knowing it, might have concerned him. It would not be difficult to go a good deal further along this irrational course: the words "without their knowing it," for instance, were superfluous, for if his presence had caused them to fall silent—although they were not embarrassed to speak in front of the proprietress—it was obviously because they . . . because "he" . . . "In front of the proprietress," or rather, "with" her. And now they were pretending not to know one another. The woman stopped grinding only to refill the coffee mill. The workmen managed to keep another mouthful at the bottoms of their glasses. To all intents and purposes no one had anything to say; yet five minutes before he had seen through the window all three talking animatedly together.

The proprietress was about to pour another drink for the two men; they were wearing blue overalls, like most of the lighthouse workers. Mathias leaned his bicycle against the shopwindow, pushed open the glass door, stood against the bar next to the two workmen and ordered an apéritif. After having served him, the woman began grinding coffee. She was middle-aged, fat, imposing, self-assured. At this time of day there was no sailor in her establishment. The house in which her café was located had no upper floor. The sparkling water of the harbor could not be seen through the door.

Evidently no one had anything to say. The salesman turned toward the room. For a moment he was afraid it was all going to begin over again: three fishermen he had not noticed when he came in—a very young man and two older ones—were sitting over three glasses of red wine at one of the back tables; just then the youngest began speaking—but the noise of the coffee mill might have kept Mathias from hearing the beginning of the conversation. He cocked his ears. As usual, it was about the slump in crab sales. He turned back to the bar to finish this unidentifiable reddish drink.

THE VOYEUR|pp. 88–92.

In connection with the new French novel all the conventional fictional techniques have been reviewed. Some have been totally rejected, others maintained but modified to suit new ends or objectives. Dialogue, for instance, has undergone radical transformation. In the case of Robbe-Grillet it emerges from the text as lines spoken in a film. The setting for the following is a plantation veranda. The camera moves in on the characters, who speak a few of their lines. But before they have progressed very far, the author decides to summarize the bulk of the scene, merely indicating the nature of the conversation as if he were preparing a scenario. Up to the reader to imagine the rest until he encounters Franck's final line, which is the signal to cut. What Robbe-Grillet achieves by this apparently off-hand dismissal of significant dialogue is increased concentration of his jealousy theme. The mood is established, the personalities revealed, essential information imparted. Fortuitous and distracting babble is avoided on the one hand; on the other, the contrived "significant" speeches of the conventional novel. Franck's brief remark at the end heightens the reader's curiosity about the novel and suggests an ominous parallel with the actual drama being prepared for on the porch.

In the hollow of the valley, on the log bridge that crosses the little stream, there is a man crouching, facing the opposite hillside. He is a native, wearing blue trousers and a colorless undershirt that leaves his shoulders bare. He is leaning toward the liquid surface as if he were trying to see something in the muddy water.

In front of him, on the opposite bank, stretches a trapezoid-shaped patch, the side along the bank curved, all of whose banana trees have been harvested more or less recently. It is easy to count their stumps, the cut trunks leaving a short stub with a disc-shaped scar, white or yellowish depending upon its freshness. Counting by rows, there are: from left to right twenty-three, twenty-two, twenty-two, twenty-one, twenty-one, twenty, twenty-one, twenty, twenty, etc. . . . .

Beside each white disc, but in various directions, has grown the replacing sprout. Depending on the precocity of the first stem, this new plant is now between a foot and a half and a yard in height.

A . . . has just brought out the glasses, the two bottles, and the ice bucket. She begins serving: the cognac in the three glasses, then the soda, and finally three transparent ice cubes, each of which imprisons a bundle of silver needles in its heart.

"We'll be leaving early," Franck says.

"What do you mean—early?"

"Six o'clock, if you can make it."

"Six! My goodness. . . ."

"Too early for you?"

"Oh no." She laughs. Then, after a pause, "In fact, it'll be fun."

They sip their drinks.

"If all goes well," Franck says, "we'll be in town by ten and have an hour or two before lunch."

"Yes, of course. I'd prefer that too," A . . . says.

They sip their drinks.

Then they change the subject. Now both of them have finished the book they have been reading for some time; their remarks can therefore refer to the book as a whole: that is, both to the outcome and to the earlier episodes (subjects of past conversations) to which this outcome gives a new significance, or to which it adds a complementary meaning.

They have never made the slightest judgment as to the novel's value, speaking instead of the scenes, events, and characters as if they were real: a place they might remember (located in Africa, moreover), people they might have known, or whose adventures someone might have told them. Their discussions have never touched on the verisimilitude, the coherence, or the quality of the narrative. On the other hand, they frequently blame the heroes for certain acts or characteristics, as they would in the case of mutual friends.

They also sometimes deplore the coincidences of the plot, saying that "things don't happen that way," and then they construct a different probable outcome starting from a new supposition, "if it weren't for that." Other possibilities are offered, during the course of the book, which lead to different endings. The variations are extremely numerous; the variations of these, still more so. They seem to enjoy multiplying these choices, exchanging smiles, carried away by their enthusiasm, probably a little intoxicated by this proliferation . . .

"But that's it, he was just unlucky enough to have come home earlier that day, and no one could have guessed he would."

Thus Franck sweeps away in a single gesture all the suppositions they had just constructed together. It's no use making up contrary possibilities, since things are the way they are: reality stays the same.

JEALOUSY|pp. 52–54.


From Joyce, the revered ancestor of the new novel, Robbe-Grillet may well have taken the idea of constructing his first work after an ancient Greek plot: *Les Gommes* (*The Erasers*) is a sort of parody of the Oedipus story. It recounts the adventure of Wallas, a government agent sent to investigate an alleged murder in a provincial city, who ends by committing the murder himself and recognizing that his victim is his own father. Throughout there are bold allusions to the Oedipus story; if the reader grasps them, however, not so Wallas, who does not understand that the drunk in the café is asking him the riddle of the Sphinx. The association between Thebes and the house of the victim also escapes him, and only the reader guesses that the eraser he is looking for is called "Oedipe." These references to the classic tale, strewn along the narrative like detective-story hints, create the awesome atmosphere of a fate tragedy without, however, carrying any of the moral or metaphysical implication of ancient myths. Robbe-Grillet uses the Oedipus story merely as a pattern—it would be absurd to deduce from it the author's concept of destiny, etc.

At one point in his meanderings, Wallas approaches a stationery store where he will be given strong clues as to the meaning and outcome of his adventure. In a manner that recalls the surrealists, Robbe-Grillet combines realism with occult symbolism: banal objects presented as if photographed become eerie symbols of prophecy.

The shopfront—plastic and aluminum—is brand new and if the left-hand window contains only a rather ordinary display of pens, note paper and school notebooks, the one on the right is designed to attract the attention of pedestrians: it represents an "artist" drawing "from nature." A dummy, dressed in a paint-spotted smock and whose face is hidden under a huge "bohemian" beard, is hard at work in front of his easel; stepping back slightly to see both his work and the model at the same time, he is putting the finishing touches on a carefully drawn landscape—which must actually be a copy of some master. It is a hill with the ruins of a Greek temple among cypress trees; in the foreground, fragments of columns lie scattered here and there; in the distance, in the valley, appears a whole city with its triumphal arches and palaces—rendered, despite the distance and the accumulation of buildings, with a scrupulous concern for detail. But in front of the man, instead of the Greek countryside, stands instead of the setting a huge photographic reproduction of a modern city intersection. The nature of this image and its skillful arrangement give the panorama a reality all the more striking in that it is the negation of the drawing supposed to represent it; and suddenly Wallas recognizes the place: that house surrounded by huge apartment buildings, that iron fence, that spindle-tree hedge, is the corner of the Rue des Arpenteurs. Obviously.

Wallas walks in.

"Well," he exclaims, "you certainly have a strange window!"

"It's interesting, isn't it?"

The young woman greets him with a low, throaty laugh.

"It certainly is strange," Wallas admits.

"Did you recognize it? Those are the ruins of Thebes."

"The photograph is particularly surprising. Don't you think so?"

"Oh yes. It's a very fine photo."

Her expression actually indicates that she sees nothing remarkable about it. But Wallas would like to know more:

"Yes, indeed," he says, "you can tell it's the work of an expert."

"Yes, of course. I had the enlargement made by a laboratory that specializes in such things."

"And the shot had to be extremely clear too."

"Yes, probably."

Already the saleswoman is looking at him with a professionally friendly expression of interrogation. "Can I help you?"

"I'd like an eraser," Wallas says.

"Yes. What kind of eraser?"

That's just the whole point, and Wallas once again begins describing what he is looking for: a soft, crumbly gum eraser that friction doesn't twist but reduces to dust; an eraser that cuts easily and whose cut surface is shiny and smooth, like mother of pearl. He has seen one such, a few months ago, at a friend's but the friend couldn't tell him where it came from. He thought he could find himself one of the same kind without difficulty, but he's been searching in vain ever since. It looked like a yellowish cube, about an inch or two long, with the corners slightly rounded—maybe by use. The manufacturer's brand was printed on one side, but was too worn to be legible any more: only two of the middle letters were still clear: "di"; there must have been at least two letters before and perhaps two or three others after.

*THE ERASERS* | from a forthcoming translation by Richard Howard.

### REFERENCES

Barthes, Roland. "Littérature objective," *Critique*, July–August, 1954. Translated by Richard Howard as "Alain Robbe-Grillet," *Evergreen Review*, II, 5 (1958), 113–126.

Blanchot, Maurice. "Notes sur un roman," *La Nouvelle Revue Française,* July, 1955, pp. 105–112.

Barthes, Roland. "Littérature littérale," *Critique,* September–October, 1955, pp. 820–826.

Dort, Bernard. "Sur les romans de Robbe-Grillet," *Les Temps Modernes,* June, 1957, pp. 1989–1999.

Morrissette, Bruce. "Surfaces et structures dans les romans de Robbe-Grillet," *The French Review,* April, 1958, pp. 364–369.

Brée, Germaine. "Jalousie: New Blinds or Old," *Yale French Studies,* 24 (Summer, 1959), pp. 87–90.

Morrissette, Bruce. "En relisant Robbe-Grillet," *Critique,* July, 1959, pp. 579–608.

Morrissette, Bruce. "New Structure in the Novel: *Jealousy,* by Alain Robbe-Grillet," *Evergreen Review,* III, 10 (1959), 103–107, 164–190.

Mauriac, Claude. *L'Alittérature contemporaine.* Translated as *New Literature.*

Morrissette, Bruce. "Oedipus and Existentialism: *Les Gommes* of Robbe-Grillet," *Wisconsin Studies in Contemporary Literature,* I, 3 (1961), 43–73.

Pingaud, Bernard. *Ecrivains d'aujourd'hui.*

SELECTED WORKS

*Tropismes* (Denoël, 1939). Republished by Editions de Minuit, 1957.

*Portrait d'un inconnu* (Robert Marin, 1947). Republished by Gallimard, 1956. Preface by Jean-Paul Sartre. Translated by Maria Jolas as *Portrait of a Man Unknown* (Braziller, 1958).

*Martereau* (Gallimard, 1953). Translated by Maria Jolas (Braziller, 1959).

*Le Planétarium* (Gallimard, 1959). Translated by Maria Jolas as *The Planetarium* (Braziller, 1960).

*L'Ere du Soupçon* (Gallimard, 1956).

"Rebels in a World of Platitudes," *The Times Literary Supplement*, June 10, 1960, p. 371.

# NATHALIE SARRAUTE

Born in Russia in 1902, Nathalie Sarraute has lived in Paris since the age of five. She attended several foreign universities including Oxford where she spent a year, and holds the *licence* in letters and in law. Married to a prominent Parisian lawyer, she practiced law herself until 1939. She is the mother of three married daughters, who pursue careers in the arts—theater criticism, films, and commercial art.

Mme. Sarraute's fame dates from 1956–1957, when Gallimard reissued her ten-year-old *Portrait d'un inconnu* and the Editions de Minuit brought out an even earlier work, *Tropismes.* Doubtless it was her essay on the art of fiction, *L'Ere du Soupçon* (1956), which directed public attention first to Mme. Sarraute and aroused general curiosity to read her creative work. Condemning in vigorous and picturesque language the novel techniques of the past, especially the "psychological" tradition, she took a place alongside Robbe-Grillet as a leader in the advance guard. Her situation is somewhat paradoxical in the eyes of her critics, for this enemy of "psychology" in the novel has been called the greatest French psychologist since Proust. Her earlier pieces are extremely subtle mood poems that depict imprecise and constantly fluctuating states of being, often far below consciousness. They are but exercises, however, compared to her latest work, *Le Planétarium,* which stands as a real novel with techniques mastered and subjugated to serve fiction. It seems regrettable that she did not reach that mastery at an earlier age, for it is now probably too late for her to produce any imposing volume of fiction. For this reason (as well as for the reason that her talent as a novelist is extremely specialized) one could not seriously sustain a general comparison with Marcel Proust. She follows Proust, but as a gleaner.

If the quality of her psychological delvings and demonstrations has brought to mind Proust, her manner recalls rather several other novelists. From Jean-Paul Sartre, with whom she must be on very good personal terms, she has taken a whole vocabulary of visceral and viscous terms; from Dostoievsky, the crouching, cringing character, hypersensitive to the impression he makes on others and to his own ignominy; from Virginia Woolf, narrative techniques and structure; from Ivy Compton-Burnett, the art of conversation.

Nathalie Sarraute's ambition to render fleeting awarenesses, psychological states which lie deep below articulate speech, leads her to employ an extraordinary imagery based on the most rudimentary animal forms. Here is a procession of those unhappy women whom Henry de Montherlant might call "celles que l'on ne prend pas dans ses bras" as they appear in the consciousness of the hero, the "family neurotic."

They wait behind doors. They ring. The family neurotic, curled up at the foot of the bed, ensconced at the far end of his room which looks out on a damp little courtyard, hears their ring. He had been waiting for it, his eyes glued to the clock: a sharp, short ring which never comes late, but rather on the early side, always inclined to be five minutes ahead of time. He recognizes it right away: furtive, slightly urgent and already aggressive, relentless. A sharp, cold little ring, which is repeated at regular, calmly calculated intervals, as often as is needed to get an answer.

There they stand behind the door. Waiting. He feels them unfolding, creeping insidiously towards him. They grope about. They aim their suckers towards the sensitive, vital spot in him, knowing exactly where it is.

Except for him, nobody sees them standing ponderously in the doorways, like pot-bellied tumbler dolls weighted down with lead, which always straighten up again if laid flat, thrown to the ground or knocked over. They always straighten up again. No matter whether you scratch or bite them, throw them out shouting, shake them or hurl them downstairs —they get up again, a little sore, give a pat to the pleats in their skirts, and back they come.

Nobody identifies them as they walk past, very proper, with trim hat and gloves. They refasten their gloves carefully in the vestibule before ringing the door bell. On summer afternoons, the concierges, seated in the doorways to get a bit of fresh air, watch them walk by: grandmothers who are not allowed to see their grandchildren as often as they should, daughters who go to see their old fathers at least twice a week, all kinds of neglected women, maltreated women, who have come to explain their case.

Formerly, when they were still quite young, much less resistant and less robust, a trained eye would have been able to pick them out—already avid and ponderous, already weighted down with lead—watching and waiting, on the plush chairs at the dancing class, or in ballrooms, or in the casinos at fashionable resorts, seated beside their parents, around little tables at tea time. A sort of thick, acrid substance exuded from them like sweat or grease. All kinds of creeping, gnawing little desires uncoiled in them like tiny snakes, nests of vipers, worms: hidden, corrosive desires, somewhat like those of Madame Bovary. They watched smartly dressed young men who also strongly resembled those Madame Bovary had noticed in the ballrooms of her day, gliding past over polished floors. These young men had the same manner, the same airy, supple way of holding their heads; they, too, let their indifferent glance rove at random; they had the same expression of aloof, rather dull-witted satisfaction. The tentacles that issued already from the girls, the little sucking, groping valves, hardly grazed them. They felt, at the most, a sort of tickling, as though gossamer threads had brushed them, clinging to their clothes, threads which they shed without being aware of them, as they went on their way. The girls watched them glide close by, unseeing, staring into space with their fashionably expressionless, cold fisheyes, moving unerringly away, guided by mysterious, indeterminable currents.

Later, in their beds at night, the damsels would weep and wring their hands, trying to understand, imploring Providence. . . .

But little by little they had gained experience and assurance. With the almost imperceptible, delicate movements of a bird, the infallible instinct that causes it to sort out exactly what is needed to build its nest, they had succeeded, little by little, in picking up, here and there, from everything that came to hand, bits and scraps which they had put together to build themselves a soft little nest, within which they stayed, well protected, watched over on every side, well sheltered.

It was extraordinary to see with what rapidity, skill and voracious tenacity they caught on the wing, managed to extract from everything, books, plays, films, a quite unimportant conversation, a random phrase, a proverb, a song, pictures, chromos—*Childhood, Maternity, Pastoral Scenes, The Joys of Home,* or even subway posters and advertisements, the principles laid down by manufacturers of soap powders and face creams ("How to hold a husband . . ."), the advice of Aunt Annie or Father Soury—it was extraordinary to see how unfailingly, among all

NATHALIE SARRAUTE | **127**

the things that came to hand, they seized upon exactly what was needed to spin their cocoon, their impermeable covering, to fashion this armor in which later on, under the kindly eye of the concierges, they went forth— amid general encouragement, unconquerable, calm and assured: grand-mothers, daughters, maltreated women, mothers—standing at doors, pressing with all their weight against doors, like heavy battering rams.

Now and then, when I have been seated next to them at the theatre, without looking at them, while they listened motionless and as though turned to stone beside me, I have sensed the trail left across the entire audience in the wake of the images emanating from the stage or from the screen, images that settle on them like steel filings on a magnetic surface; I longed to rise, to intervene and check these images in their flight, to turn them aside; but they flowed with an irresistible force, straight from the screen onto the women; they clung to them; and I felt the women close beside me, in the darkness of the hall, motionless, silent and voracious, spinning these images into an object destined for their own use.

PORTRAIT OF A MAN UNKNOWN | pp. 40–43.

"L'enfer c'est les autres," said Jean-Paul Sartre, and Mme. Sarraute concerns herself particularly with the exquisite sufferings endured by human beings in the presence of others. Sarraute's wretched specimens of humanity find titillation, even voluptuousness in their torment—as in this sadistic *pas de deux*.

If she had ever raised her head in disdain and cast an absent-minded gaze elsewhere, perhaps the beast in him—like a dog that stops barking and retires, calmed down, when the passer-by he was attacking goes on his way, unperturbed—perhaps the beast in him would have fallen asleep again; but he saw her there at his feet, cringing, crawling in the mud and the mire; there she was before him, flaccid, acquiescent, always within reach; the temptation was too great, an irresistible desire was growing in him to seize hold of her, to bend her double, to batter her down, further still, harder . . . "But my poor girl, I know you, a gold mine, El Dorado itself, do you hear me, all the gold of Croesus, nothing would change you, I could give you anything on earth, you would still deprive yourself of everything, you would let yourself die of hunger, just to be able to put more and more money aside . . . you like to do it, I know you, you're like that, you can't do without it . . ."

"Well, I must say, that's going too far . . . !" All at once her eyes filled with tears. ". . . that's really too hard . . ." She was on the verge of a scene, she had that air of helpless anger of a child who is about to "go into a tantrum"—"You dare say that to me, it's you who say that to me! That's going too far! You know perfectly well"—all at once she had softened, her eyes were streaming—"you know perfectly well I wouldn't be like that if I had been brought up differently, you are the one who gave me the habit . . ." Her flat face and dejected air gave her the look of a weeping widow . . . She did it on purpose, it was to make him feel ashamed, he knew that, in order to humiliate him, to make people feel sorry for her at his expense, that she got herself up the way she did, with her black lisle-thread stockings and her darned gloves, so that she could throw that into his face: you made me what I am, you wanted it, I am your product, your handiwork . . .

He could have taken her in his two hands and crushed her. . . . "Ah! so it's me now, so I'm the cause of all your woes, I'm your scapegoat. . . . I can tell you I'm beginning to have about enough—I've shouldered the blame for too long, I've had enough. . . ." He was hesitating, he was looking around him for something to crush her with, but there was nothing within reach, he found nothing at hand, except such coarse, heavy-to-handle contrivances as are used by the people up there—he sensed confusedly that this was not what was needed here, between them, they didn't need crude instruments borrowed from those other people out there, but it couldn't be helped, he saw nothing else, he had no choice. . . . "You ought to look around a bit, catch yourself another victim. . . . Find yourself a husband, what the hell. . . . A husband. . . . It's high time. . . ." He felt that he was crushing a flabby substance that was yielding and into which he was sinking. . . . "When you need that badly to be carried along on somebody's outstretched arms, or live like a parasite, always clinging to somebody else, you look for a husband. A husband. . . . Then it would be his turn. . . . Only . . ." he was sinking further and further down, he was being dragged down, meeting with no resistance . . . "only, there's nobody around, eh? nobody wants the job, I take it! Ah, ha! there haven't been any bidders yet . . ." he was experiencing the painful, sickening voluptuousness of a maniac, the kind that takes one's breath away, that one feels when one presses one's own abscess between two fingers to make the pus spurt out, or when one tears off bit by bit the scab of a wound . . . "they don't want the job, they're no fools . . ." he was choking, his words came with difficulty . . . "for them there's nothing doing . . ." he was going down, he was sinking as though from dizziness, drawn further and further down, to the depths of a strange voluptuousness, a funny sort of voluptuousness that resembled suffering: "Ah! it's because she's too homely, if you must know . . . she's too homely . . . and it's probably I too, I who forced you . . . I who am responsible for your looks. . . ."

She struggled feebly, gave a few kicks without really trying to disengage herself, hitting out the while in a mild way that increased his excitement; she started talking in her weepy, slightly childish, exasperating voice. . . . "Yes, it's you, of course it's you, you did everything you could to keep me by myself, so that I should see nobody, you always kept me from seeing people, or going out . . . what scenes you used to make if I ever made so bold as to invite anyone for dinner . . . I looked like a servant girl, I was dressed like a servant girl, I didn't dare let anybody see me. . . ." He took a little time off to tighten his hold, get a more convenient grip on her, he had all the time he needed, there she was in his hands, inert, one might have said that she was waiting. . . . He sneered . . . "Naturally . . . I was sure of it . . . that's nothing new . . . I'm the unfeeling brute . . . I'm the ogre who kept the suitors from crowding around to sue for happiness . . ." One moment more . . . before letting himself fall further down, to the bottom this time, to the very bottom. . . . "No, my poor girl, just between ourselves, eh? No, but can't you see for yourself, tell me, have you ever looked at yourself . . ." the abscess had burst, the scab was entirely off, the wound was bleeding, suffering and voluptuousness had attained their peak, he was at the end of his tether, at the very end, they had reached bottom, alone together, they were by themselves, now they were quite by themselves, naked, stripped, far from outside eyes . . . he felt steeped in the atmosphere of mellowness, the relaxed tepidity produced by intimacy—alone in their nice, big hideout, where you can do anything you want, where there is no longer any need to conceal anything—he was holding her by the lapel of her coat, talking right close up to her face. . . . "Well, if you want to know, I never did speak to you about it, but since you force me to do so now, well, I'm going to tell you . . . if you want to know the truth, I did everything, I tell you, everything and more still. . . . You remember that Adonis, that young fellow . . . you know perfectly well who I'm talking about . . . well, I all but crawled to get him to marry you, I made up to him, I even went so far as to sink money in that little business of his . . . but as for him, there was nothing doing . . . he left, you remember. . . ." He looked at her a bit from one side, his voice was slightly hoarse. . . . "He left, he cut and ran . . . in other words, nothing came of it. . . ."

PORTRAIT OF A MAN UNKNOWN|pp. 185–189.

The mother of the young bride is contemplating the present of a pair of sturdy leather chairs to the young couple. But her "arty" son-in-law has his heart set on an antique *bergère*. The situation, as it takes shape in her consciousness, is rendered in a manner that owes greatly to Virginia Woolf and Marcel Proust.

It's extraordinary how she feels these things in advance. It's a source of wonder each time, to find that everything that was going to happen was already there in the bud, she had felt it at the moment, she knew that it was there, all ready, foreshadowed, she had sensed it quite clearly, she never makes a mistake, everything was going to come out of that and unroll, as astonishingly for the innocent on-looker as those long rolls of paper, the ribbon that keeps coming out of the magician's hat: everything that had already happened, everything that's coming now, came from the following brief question: she had hesitated to ask it, she had turned away . . . watch out, we mustn't allow ourselves to be tempted, let's forget it, Lord knows what that might stir up . . . But her friends—how could they have guessed it? how could sane, normal people think it?—her friends, in their simplicity, in their guilelessness, had encouraged her: "You're looking at our new easy-chairs. They're nice, aren't they? We've got a little upholsterer who does perfect work . . . He furnishes only the best quality of leather . . . He used to work for Maple and has now gone into business for himself . . . It's as well finished as at Maple's . . . Extremely sturdy . . . And much less expensive . . . You ought to tell your children about him, since they're fixing up their apartment. This will last them all their lives . . ." And that was true: it was exactly what they needed, what she would have liked to give them—robust, long-wearing, magnificent leather. She had run her hand along the arm, she had felt the cushion, springy, silky, the back comfortably and simply shaped, in the best English taste . . . But there was no use asking the address. That's not for us, all that kind of thing, not for such as us out there. Here everything is as reliable as these chairs, everything is simple, clean-cut. But out there, at her daughter's . . . shadows, dark holes, disquieting swarmings, soft uncoilings, dangerous layers of ooze that open up, engulf her . . . it's enough for her to set foot there, it's enough for her to say a word, to give her advice, for her merely to pronounce the name of her friends, and right away it never fails: silent withdrawals, contained shrugs, hardly perceptible ironic smiles, exchange of looks . . . no . . . she's too frightened . . . she prefers to remain apart, avoid all temptation, not stick her finger in the machinery, turn aside . . . But her friends keep after her: "Now do look at them. They're really the very best quality. And if we told you the price . . . Guess, how much would you say? . . ." She shakes her head with an air of appraisal, amazed: "Ah! that really is dirt cheap."

NATHALIE SARRAUTE | **131**

But they're ridiculous, after all, those ideas of hers . . . Nervousness—she'll dismiss all that. It's she, her excessive tact, her fits of diffidence with them, the desire that seizes her all of a sudden to curry favor with them, to get them to like her, which makes them that way . . . Her friends would certainly say that if she spoke to them about it: they're just a pair of kids . . . kids with no experience, excessively spoilt, rotten, rich kids who've never done anything except what they wanted . . . what's all this about, what are all these flickering shadows, these troubled waters, these disquieting reactions . . . She should be with them as she is with other people: be someone who is quite simple, straightforward, frank, not be afraid: they'll pretty well accept what's given them, that would be the last straw . . . and delighted at that . . . life will teach them . . . they are very comfortable, these chairs are, and there's no use smiling on the side of your faces and looking at each other like that, you'll be glad enough one of these days, when you're a little older, when you'll be working harder, when you'll be more tired than you are now, to sit down in these easy-chairs . . . they'll last forever, they certainly will, and that's important, believe it or not, ask your father, he was the one who earned the money to buy them with . . . Yes, we're going to be like everybody else, we too, they're completely ridiculous, when all's said and done, all these complications, these finicky tastes, we're going to be like my friends here who look at me with their good, innocent eyes: "Why don't you have a pair made like that for your daughter and her husband? They are really a bargain.—Why not, true enough, you're right. What's the name of your upholsterer? Let me have his address for my daughter. They're exactly what she needs . . ."

What could be simpler, more natural? A mother filled with solicitude—and what had she not done for this child, what wouldn't she do?—gives her daughter and son-in-law the address of a good upholsterer, makes them a present of two handsome easy-chairs . . . "Exactly what you need, you won't find anything better. I got the address through the Perrins, you can tell him they sent you. He used to work for Maple. He will give you a special price. They are comfortable, sturdy and very pretty . . . made of splendid leather." But it's doubtless her voice, something in the tone, in the sound of her voice, a note of hesitation, of uneasiness, a lack of self-confidence, which must have set everything going. They are like dogs that grow excited from fear, even when it's hidden, they feel it . . . it was that barely perceptible waver in her voice, which started everything, which upset everything . . . they hesitated a moment, they looked at each other . . . "Oh, thank you Maman—we want, Alain and I . . . We had thought we should like to have an authentic *bergère*, we saw one in an antique shop . . . It will be a little more ex-

pensive perhaps than the leather chairs, but I assure you, it, too, is a bargain, and it's so much prettier . . ." These words, apparently harmless
—but only the uninitiated could make this mistake—these words, like
those that once revealed heresy and led directly to the stake, showed that
the evil was still there, as alive and strong as ever . . . her heart started
to beat, she blushed, anybody else, except them, would have been surprised
by the violence of her reaction, the hatred, the rage in her tone all of a
sudden, in her false, icy laughter, she herself felt sick when she heard it:
"Oh, how stupid of me . . . I keep forgetting . . . that's true . . . it's
enough for it to come from me, poor fool that I am . . . or for it to come
from friends of mine . . . I knew it, I didn't even want to ask them for
the address . . . But I couldn't resist, it was such a bargain . . . I
should have bought them for us, if I could have done so just
now . . ." The look they gave each other . . . They always have awful
looks . . . their eyes seek each other out, find each other right away, become motionless, stare, stretched wide, as though they were full to splitting.
She knows what composes this silent transfusion that takes place up above
her while she lies prone between them, powerless, inert, floored: it's there,
eh? We were right. Did you see that? I did. Congratulations, that was
certainly the reaction that had been foreseen. We are very clever. It's
exactly as we thought, it's what we always say . . . she has to call the
tune . . . as soon as you take a step off the path chosen by her, she sets
herself up as a flouted victim . . . She's bossy . . . possessive . . . She
gives in order to dominate . . . to keep us forever under her tutelage
. . . And that little pique at the end . . . Did you notice that?—I did
. . . To hear her tell it, she takes the bread out of her own mouth to
give to us . . . her eternal sacrifices . . . What play-acting . . . She
feels a faintness, a dull pain . . . She shouldn't have . . . But they are
the ones who drive her to do these things, to say things like that to them,
now she's ashamed, she was already ashamed at the moment, but they are
the ones who cause her to slip, who make her step in that dirt, that mire
. . . what he calls "those little marshes". . . He detects them right
away. He sees everything . . . always on the watch . . . and he shows
them to her, to her own daughter, to her little girl, who hadn't seen a
thing: that clear gaze of hers, so pure, formerly, so confiding, there was
nothing lovelier than her mama, but he, he spies, he hunts, he finds and
he shows everybody: "Right this way . . . is there anybody who hasn't
got his little recesses . . ." And she, pitiful, crazy old woman, ridiculous
. . . smiling away . . . wriggling . . . oh no, you mustn't believe
. . . you're mistaken, I assure you . . . there's none of all that about me,
you must believe me, nothing except a real doting mama, continual little
treats, presents, better than a mother—a friend. But he won't be taken in.
No use to kick. With a firm hand, he holds the mask which he had plas-
tered down on her face from the very first, that grotesque, outmoded mask
of the vaudeville mother-in-law, of the old woman who sticks her nose

into everything, the tyrant who keeps her daughter and son-in-law well in hand.

THE PLANETARIUM|pp. 46–51.

## REFERENCES

Audry, Colette. "Nathalie Sarraute, communication et reconnaissance," *Critique*, January, 1954, pp. 14–19.

Sartre, Jean-Paul. Preface to *Portrait d'un inconnu* translated by Beth Brombert as "The Anti-Novel of Nathalie Sarraute," *Yale French Studies*, 16 (Winter, 1955–1956), pp. 40–44.

Robbe-Grillet, Alain. "Le réalisme, la psychologie et l'avenir du roman," *Critique*, August–September, 1956, pp. 695–701.

Bourdet, Denise. "Nathalie Sarraute," *La Revue de Paris*, June, 1958, pp. 127–130.

Mauriac, Claude. *L'Alittérature contemporaine*. Translated as *New Literature*.

Serreau, Geneviève. "Nathalie Sarraute nous parle du *Planétarium*," *Les Lettres Nouvelles*, April 29, 1959, pp. 28–30.

Minor, Anne. "Nathalie Sarraute: Le Planétarium," *Yale French Studies*, 24 (Summer, 1959), pp. 96–100.

Minor, Anne. "Nathalie Sarraute," *The French Review*, December, 1959, pp. 107–115.

Toynbee, Philip. "A pronoun too few," *The Times Literary Supplement*, January 1, 1960, pp. 1–2.

Pingaud, Bernard. *Ecrivains d'aujourd'hui.*

Matthews, John H. "Nathalie Sarraute: an approach to the novel," *Modern Fiction Studies*, VI, 4 (Winter, 1960–1961), 334–337.

## SELECTED WORKS

*Le Tricheur* (Sagittaire, 1945). Subsequently republished by Editions de Minuit.

*La Corde raide* (Sagittaire, 1947). Subsequently republished by Editions de Minuit. *Gulliver* (Calmann-Lévy, 1952).

*Le Sacre du Printemps* (Calmann-Lévy, 1954).

*Le Vent* (Editions de Minuit, 1957). Translated by Richard Howard as *The Wind* (Braziller, 1959).

*L'Herbe* (Editions de Minuit, 1958). Translated by Richard Howard as *The Grass* (Braziller, 1960).

*La Route des Flandres* (Editions de Minuit, 1960). Translated by Richard Howard as *The Flanders Road* (Braziller, 1961).

*Le Palace* (Editions de Minuit, 1962).

"L'Attentat," *La Nouvelle Revue Française,* March, 1962.

# CLAUDE SIMON

Claude Simon, born October 10, 1913, at Tananarive, Madagascar, was a winegrower near Perpignan before he entered literature, but he now lives most of the year in Paris. The most Faulknerian of a whole generation of French writers inspired by American novelists, Simon has created a universe as dominated by fatality as Faulkner's Yoknapatawpha County and has adopted most of the devices used by his model. However great is his debt to Faulkner, he gives the appearance, at least, of indebtedness to Camus as well. *Le Tricheur*, his first novel (1945), was so reminiscent of *L'Etranger* (*The Stranger*) that Simon must have felt called upon to insist that his work was written quite independently. In *La Corde raide,* his second novel (1947), he declared that he disapproved of all preoccupation with technique and that he was not impressed by the philosophy of the absurd. His novels have revealed, however, that he is very much interested in technique, making great use of the interior monologue and, especially in his later works, taking pains to maintain the consistent point of view. His heroes are outsiders like Meursault, and all his characters testify to the author's strong penchant towards the philosophy of the absurd. Their common enemy in nature is Time, as invincible as it is incomprehensible, for man is moved by forces and for reasons that he cannot understand. By means of a heavily sensuous imagery that makes his style unique among the new novels, Simon creates a cosmic atmosphere of doom and bewilderment to enshroud mankind. Man's ultimate defeat is a sort of victory, however, since it is release and liberation whereas nature must go on without rest or end.

The new novelist's concern in maintaining the single point of view is well illustrated by Claude Simon. In *The Grass* his narrator Louise carries most of the novel by monologue, the action and characters reaching us indirectly through this device. The following passage is a portion of a scene between her parents-in-law Sabine and Pierre. Louise reports it as she overhears and imagines it; not once does the author avail himself of what would once have been considered his right, that of passing through the door to be an unseen witness of the scene.

We may feel that the new novelists concern themselves overmuch with this matter and sometimes strain painfully to maintain the single post of observation; however, here the scene is unquestionably heightened and made more dramatic by not being witnessed directly. Pierre's ancient sister is dying in another room; against the background of her labored breathing, fragments of the quarrel as to whether she should have the sacraments come through the wall to Louise's ear, inciting her to imagine this weird and awful scene between her drunken mother-in-law and Pierre, whose will is still strong although his body has become a helpless mass of obese flesh. In sentences characteristic of the author that run over pages, an elaborate allusion to opera is extended, making up an imagined scene more vivid than any real one. Simon is no enemy of metaphor as Robbe-Grillet professes to be. His style is rich in sensual imagery which often becomes, as here, wildly exuberant.


Louise able to hear her, to imagine her standing in the doorway, probably half dressed, a piece of clothing (or a brush, or a comb) in one hand—the hand covered with cold cream and loaded with rings—, standing in that kind of aureole (as if it emanated from her, even when she was motionless, like a permanent and indecent tinkling of jewels, of bracelets clashing), with her red hair, her faded, painted face, her vulnerable flesh resembling, in the ample, diaphanous and silky night-gown, some character in opera, some old dishevelled prima donna, bejewelled, mad and half naked, incarnating some pathetic protest, some pathetic and unequal combat lost beforehand (both by the character and by herself, ceaselessly repeating the same and terrifying Farewell Performance in which she stubbornly, blindly repeats the role, the success, the travesty of herself at twenty, aphonic, fleshless, exhibiting her sagging old breasts in the decolleté gown), lost against time, so that Louise had no need to hear distinctly what he said in order to know, to foresee the failure, the old man's answer repeated a second time, slowly, calmly: "No!"

She stood motionless, holding her breath, listening to the two invisible, muffled, but distinct voices alternate, answering each other—as if they reached her not simply muted by the interposition of a thin layer of bricks, but from a great distance in space or time, this perspective conferring upon them a new kind of existence, distilling them, stripping them of everything that in reality (the direct contact with reality) disturbs our perception, the latter usually being solicited from all sides, scattered, dispersed—, the two people, then, reduced to only their voices, to their principles, so to speak, their essentials, the voice with the prima donna's doleful and pathetic inflections colliding with the other's pachydermous, exhausted, patient, and unshakable opposition.

"But since she won't know anything, she won't even notice, she's unconscious . . . So you're going to let your sister, your own sister die like a dog, as if she were nothing more than a dog, an animal, when she probably wouldn't even realize, it only takes a few minutes, just the time to put a little oil on her face and feet and say a . . ."

"I told you, no."

"So you forbid me, you . . ."

"It's not me, it's Marie, that's the way she's always wanted it, you know that as well as . . ."

"It's not Marie, since she can't feel anything, can't see anything any more, can't even say anything, who can say, who can know or even guess what she's thinking at this very moment, suppose she's changed her mind, how can you know if she doesn't want it now, what would she say if she could talk, no one in this house has ever died like that before, so now, when it's your own sister, then they'll come and get her just like that, they'll take her away and put her in the ground like garbage, something to get rid of by burning it and shovelling the dirt over it . . . Are you listening to me?" Stopping then, the flood of words suspended, Louise able to see her, imagine her, motionless in the theatrical pose of an old diva, awaiting, expecting—no, not even that, not even applause any more, and perhaps not even acquiescence: only a sign, an indication, attention— and on her face that somewhat distracted expression, that same panic of an old Walkyrie glittering with jewels or rather (in the shiny yellow decor of the bathroom papered with Japanese birds and cherry branches in bloom) the Madama Butterfly in her brilliant kimono, with her ravaged, ruined mask, reaching, breathless, the place, the note where once the thunder of cheers, the ovations broke loose, her eyes searching the half-empty house, a few subscribers dozing in the orchestra, all of whom have been to bed with her and have long since stopped being interested (both in going to bed with and listening to, even younger singers), Sabine, then, standing among the snow of spring flowers, the eternal and soundless cheeping of the exotic birds perched on the red branches, and he, probably half-naked too (or undressing, for suddenly she said: "Now you know you can't do that by yourself, here, wait a mi . . ." and he: "Yes," and she: "Now the other one . . . Of course you're caught now, you always do it that way . . . Wait till I find . . . There, that's it), mountainous, probably sitting down, and she leaning over him now, perhaps buttoning up the pajama jacket over the enormous naked belly with its strangely white, strangely delicate, vulnerable and disarming skin, Louise still standing in front of her reflection staring back at her in that sort of double solitude, vigilant, motionless, the jar of cold cream—or perhaps the brush now—still in her hand, motionless, not from fear of making a noise, of being heard and not even to hear better (any more than the old, exhausted and still assiduous subscribers: probably because the voice—or the absence of voice—of the old, broken-down prima donna is not so much the object of their fidelity or of, simply, their presence, any more than their interest in the characters which she is supposed to incarnate, the long and ectoplasmic series of gesticulating and shrieking heroines majestically parading their trains, their crowns, and their false jewels across the dusty boards, as the somnolent and yet unappeasable nostalgia for that something which all the howling Juliettes or Marguerites with their false braids are less likely to resuscitate than any skillful scalpel or any reinvigorating monkey graft), content then (Louise) to register mechanically, passively, the voices, the words ("And where are we going to put her, have you thought of that?"—Put her?—Yes, put her, there are only two places left, when we buried Papa there were only three, so— Well?—And what about us, where'll we go . . . I suppose I'm not even entitled to be with my own family, where all my relatives have always . . . —But there'll still be one place left—And what about you?—Oh I don't care what you do with me, you . . ."), able to see the orchestra conductor's magic wand conjure up the traditional painted canvas spasmodically shaken by drafts from the wings (unless it was the air blown through the serpentine complication of the brasses) and on which the sempiternal and wearisome Italian cloister painted in *grisaille* serves as a background to the sempiternal cardboard tomb raised as an imperishable monument to the imperishable glory of the monkey glands in a kind of macabre apotheosis, an eternal perpetuation: the old woman no longer audible on the other side of the partition save for a vague, plaintive murmur, a kind of grievance aria, still bending over—undressing and then dressing for the night the mountainous, misshapen and impotent body like some ridiculous ghost of his youth, watching ahead of time, perhaps, her own funeral, probably dimly imagining a kind of after-life in the form of a vague subterranean existence where she and the old man would find themselves finally and perfectly reunited . . .

THE GRASS|pp. 139–144.

The traditional business of the novel has been to show that things are not what they seem to be, to show that the smooth round entities which persons, things, and ideas appear to be are not really so at all. Often, with lesser novelists especially, this has meant however substituting one smooth, round entity for another —a character is thought to be an honest man, the author shows that he is a crook instead. Greater novelists have always left their characters ambiguous and have avoided giving too precise or absolute interpretation of events. Today, however, with writers like Claude Simon, there can be no question at all of a whole truth or a proper interpretation immutable and absolute. The novelist's search for reality ends in a realization that it is nowhere but in its own denial, in partial knowledge, error, and subjective perception.

And while the notary was talking, telling the story again for maybe the tenth time (or at least what he knew of the story, or what he imagined, having, in relation to the events which had occurred during the last seven months, like everyone else, like the heroes of those events, only that fragmentary, incomplete knowledge consisting of an accretion of sudden images (and those only partially apprehended by the sense of sight) or an accumulation of words (themselves poorly grasped) or a welter of generally ill-defined sensations, and everything—words, images, sensations—vague, full of gaps, blanks that the imagination and an approximative logic tried to remedy by a series of risky deductions—risky though not necessarily false: because either everything is only chance and then the thousand and one versions, the thousand and one appearances of a story are also a story, or rather are and constitute *the* story, since that's the way it is and was and remains in the consciousness of the people who lived it, suffered it, endured it, laughed at it; or else reality is endowed with a life of its own, disdainful and independent of our perceptions and consequently of our knowledge and especially of our thirst for logic— and in that case trying to find it, discover it, drive it out of hiding is perhaps just as futile and disappointing as those toys, those Central European dolls that look like old women cupped one within the other, each enclosing, revealing a smaller one inside, until you get down to something minute, infinitesimal, insignificant . . . nothing at all; and now, now that it's all over, trying to report, to reconstitute what happened is a little like trying to stick together the scattered, incomplete debris of a broken mirror, clumsily struggling to readjust the pieces, getting only an incoherent, ridiculous, idiotic result; or perhaps only our mind or rather our pride forces us to risk madness and run counter to all the evidence just to find at any price a logical relation of cause to effect in the very world where everything the reason manages to make out is fugitive and vague, where the uncertain senses are tossed about like floating corks without direction or perspective, trying only to stay afloat, and suffering, and dying just to get it over with, and that's all . . . ) . . .

THE WIND | pp. 9–11.

Description of a battle by the eye-witness technique is often said to begin in French literature with Stendhal, who, in *The Charterhouse of Parma,* showed us the battle of Waterloo as it might have been experienced by a simple and obscure participant. Simon depicts the rout of the French armies in 1940 also by the eye-witness technique, but in a manner as different from Stendhal's as Stendhal's was from the epic technique. At first it seems to be narration, but then appears more like interior monologue and stream-of-consciousness recording. Doubtless it is a combination of all three. What passed through the soldier's mind and across his field of vision is mixed up with the account of the event which he will later make, possibly to a fellow internee as they work away on the coal pile.

I never heard the order shouted seeing only the bodies in front of me collapse closer and closer while the right legs moved one after the other over the rumps like the pages of a book flipped backward and once on the ground I looked for Wack to hand him the bridle at the same time that my right hand was struggling behind my back with that damn rifle hook then it came on us from behind the thunder of hoofs the galloping of wild horses riderless now eyes huge ears flat stirrups empty the reins whipping the air twisting like serpents and two or three covered with blood and one with his rider still on his back screaming They're behind us too they let us get through and then they, the rest of his words carried away with him leaning over the neck his mouth wide open like a hole and now it was no longer with the rifle hook that I was struggling but against that nag trying to break away head high neck stiff as a mast the pupil entirely blank as though she were trying to look behind her ears stepping back not by fits and starts but so to speak methodically one foot after the other and me pulling at her hard enough to tear off her jaw saying All right All right as if she could even hear me in that racket gradually shortening the reins until I could reach her neck with one hand patting her repeating All right All right Theeeeeere . . . until she stopped, standing motionless but tense strained trembling in every limb her hoofs stiff and wide apart like stilts and probably there had been another order shouted while I was struggling with her because I realized (not seeing because I was too busy watching her but sensing, divining) in that disorder that uproar that they were all remounting getting close to her then (still as stiff as strained as if she had been made out of wood) as gently as possible watching carefully in case she kicked or reared or broke into a gallop just when I would have a foot in the stirrup but she still didn't move just trembling where she stood like a motor idling and she let me get my foot in the stirrup without doing a thing, only when I seized the pommel and the cantle to lift myself up the saddle turned over, I was expecting that too for three days I had been trying to find a girth to exchange for this one that was too long for her after I had had to leave Edgar behind but you can't get a thing out of those peasants it was as if asking them to switch girths was trying to rob them and Blum's was too long too so it was really the perfect moment for a thing like that to happen to me when there was shooting on all sides at once but I didn't even have time to swear not even enough breath not even enough time to get out a word just enough to think of it while I was trying to get that damn saddle on her back again in the middle of all those men who were passing around me at a gallop now and then I saw that my hands were trembling but I couldn't stop them any more than I could stop her body from trembling I stopped trying I began running alongside her holding her by the bridle she starting to canter with the saddle now almost directly under her belly among the horses—with riders or riderless—that were passing us the deadly network of plucked guitar strings stretched like a ceiling over our heads but it was only when I saw two or three fall that I realized that I was in the ditch of the road while they were too high on horseback so they got shot down like ninepins then I saw Wack (things happening paradoxically enough in a kind of silence a void in other words the sound of the bullets and the explosions—they must have been using mortars now or those little tank cannons—once accepted admitted and somehow forgotten neutralizing themselves somehow you heard absolutely nothing no shouts no voices probably because no one had time to shout so that it reminded me of when I was running the 1500: only the whistling noise of the breathing the swearing itself choked before it came out and then came a jostling as if the lungs were seizing all the available air to distribute it through the body and use it only for useful things: looking deciding running, things consequently happening a little as though in a film without its sound track), I saw Wack who had just passed me leaning over the neck of his horse his face turned back toward me his mouth open too probably trying to shout something which he didn't have air enough to make heard and suddenly lifted off his saddle as if a hook an invisible hand had grabbed him by his coat collar and slowly raised him I mean almost motionless in relation to (I mean animated by almost the same speed as) his horse that kept on galloping and me still running although a little slower now so that Wack his horse and I comprised a group of objects among which the distances were modified only gradually he being now exactly over the horse from which he had just been lifted wrenched slowly rising in the air his legs still arched as though he were still riding some invisible Pegasus who had bucked and made him fall slowing then and somehow making a kind of double *salto mortale* on the spot so that I saw him next head down mouth still open on the same shout (or advice he had tried to give me) silent then lying in the air on his back like a man stretched out in a hammock and letting his legs hang down to the right and left then again head up body vertical his legs beginning to come together hanging parallel then on his stomach arms stretched forward hands open grabbing snatching something like one of those circus acrobats during the seconds when he is attached to nothing and liberated of all weight between the two trapezes then finally the head down again legs apart arms outstretched as though to bar the way but motionless now flat against the roadside slope and no longer moving staring at me his face stamped with a surprised and idiot expression I thought Poor Wack he always looked like a fool but now more than ever he, then I no longer thought, something like a mountain or a horse falling on me throwing me to the ground trampling on me while I felt the reins wrenched out of my hands then everything went black while thousands of galloping horses went on passing over my body then I no longer even felt the horses only something like a smell of ether and the dark my ears buzzing and when I opened my eyes again I was lying on the road and not one horse and only Wack still on the slope head down still looking at me his eyes wide open with that shocked look but I was careful not to move waiting for the moment when I would being [sic] to suffer having heard somewhere that the worst wounds create a kind of anesthesia at first but still feeling nothing and after a moment I tried to move but nothing happened managing to get onto my hands and knees my face toward the ground I could see the earth of the road the stones looking like triangles or irregular polygons of a slightly bluish white in their matrix of pale ochre earth there was something like a carpet of grass in the center of the path then to the right and the left where the wheels of the cars and carts passed two bare ruts then the grass growing on the sides and raising my head I saw my shadow still very pale and fantastically elongated thinking Then the sun's up, and at that moment I was aware of the silence and I saw that just beyond Wack there was a man sitting on the roadside: he was holding his arm a little above the elbow his hand hanging all red between his legs but it wasn't a man from the squadron.

THE FLANDERS ROAD|pp. 156–162.

REFERENCES

Piel, Jean. "Le Vent, Tentative de restitution d'un retable baroque," *Critique,* January, 1958, pp. 86–88.

Guicharnaud, Jacques. "Remembrance of Things Passing: Claude Simon," *Yale French Studies,* 24 (Summer, 1959), pp. 101–108.

Ricardou, Jean. "Un ordre dans le débâcle," *Critique,* December, 1960, pp. 1011–1024.

Bourin, André. "Techniciens du roman: Claude Simon," *Les Nouvelles Littéraires,* December 29, 1960.

Pingaud, Bernard. *Ecrivains d'aujourd'hui.*

SELECTED WORKS

*Soliloques,* poems, 1946.

"Nedjma," poem published in the *Mercure de France,* January 1, 1948.

"Le Cadavre encerclé," dramatic piece published in *Esprit,* December, 1954, and January, 1955, later included in *Le Cercle des représailles.*

*Nedjma,* novel (Le Seuil, 1956). Translated by Richard Howard (Braziller, 1961).

*Le Cercle des représailles,* dramatic pieces (Le Seuil, 1959).

# KATEB YACINE

Born August 26, 1929, in Condé-Smendou near Constantine, Kateb Yacine belongs to an old tribe of educated Algerians. While a student at the Collège de Sétif, he became involved in the manifestation of May 8, 1945, and was put in jail for a few months. During the following several years he cast about for a career, twice going to Paris—the first time for a nine month stay —but, unable to establish himself in the capital, he finally took a job in Algiers as reporter for the *Alger Républicain*. His assignments gave him the opportunity to see something of the Near East and more of North Africa. The death of his father in 1950 and resulting family responsibilities forced Yacine to give up journalism, remain in Algiers, and take what odd jobs he could find. However, in 1951, he was able to try his luck again in metropolitan France. In Paris he contacted his literary friends, who decided, on the basis of the promise shown by the poetry that this young North African had already published, to undertake his support for a time. Thus assured of a livelihood from 1952 to 1954, Yacine was able to complete "Le Cadavre encerclé" and establish himself as the most remarkable among the Algerians writing in French.

Critics speak of Eschylus, Faulkner, and Arabic mythology to situate this powerful new talent. It is dedicated to one theme, that of Algeria, the homeland, whose complex and passionate soul Yacine would bare by the written word. He personifies his country in the mysterious Nedjma, "born of a strange copulation of two Arabs with a Frenchwoman." In the novel, around this shadowy and motionless figure the story revolves. The four narrators have all loved her, but she has always remained beyond their reach and finally disappears completely into a mythological past. The allegory is constructed along circles:

the beginning is at any point and all progression ultimately returns to the point of departure. Yacine's powerfully poetic style, his original composition, and the grandeur of his subject have combined to place him high among the young writers today. His *Nedjma,* with its theme of chimerical quest and its circular narrative method that ignores chronology, justifies his inclusion among the new novelists.

. . . Incontestably, Nedjma's fatality derived from the atmosphere she was surrounded by as a little girl, when the already devastating games of the sacrificed Vestal glowed in her rarest adornments: the raw splendor, the streaming weapons it is incredible that a woman uses consciously, as if Lella Fatma's flatteries and the weaknesses of her husband had made the little girl into a quasi-religious object, washed clean of her childish filth, polished, inlaid, perfumed with no fear of spoiling her. The true Nedjma was wild; and her educators gradually agreed to raise all barriers before her; but this gratuitous freedom, beyond her world and her time, became the cruellest barrier of all . . . The adoptive mother was sterile, and her husband bigoted. The eunuch and the shrew, prostrate in adoration before the virgin, could harvest only hatred by their poisonous cult. Nedjma's charms, filtered by solitude, had bound her, reduced her to the contemplation of her captive beauty, to skepticism and cruelty before the dejected adoration of her guardians, having only her taciturn play, her love of darkness and jealous dreams, a batrachian full of nocturnal cries that vanished at the first ray of heat, a frog on the brink of the equation, a principle of electricity igniting every ill, after having gleamed, cried, leaped in the face of the world and crazed the male army that woman follows like a shadow it would be enough merely to cross in order to reach the zenith, far from the prolific counterpart whose product man expects only after shedding his vigor engulfed in endless experiment: the male army has embraced only a form; there remains only a collapse at the foot of the old order: male and female ready to unite at dawn, but it is a route at sunrise—the frog in the warmth of the mud, wounded in the first season and deformed for the other three, fatally bleeding at each moon, and the experimenter still virgin, still ignorant, in the despair of the vanished formula—the man and the woman mystified, deprived of their cruel substance, while outside their bodies roars the hermaphroditic horde procreating its own adversity, its males, its females, its night-long couples, from the tragic meeting on the same planet, the contradictory tribe continually emigrating for fear of other worlds too vast, too remote for human promiscuity, since watchful nature abandons us along the way; nature proceeds by errors, by crimes, to awaken the geniuses at the stake and punish those her blindness favors in some impulse of maternal naïveté, revoking all her senses and dispensing them only at random, unknown to the spawn whose stumbles she imitates, for the ingenuous mother educates best by her errors; our destinies must fall with the free leaves, once the jig-saw puzzle begins: their number condemns them to a preconceived elimination, accumulating their influence in increasingly rare champions who alone will experience, without witnesses, without memory, the confrontation with adversity; even as the nations, the tribes, the families, the operation tables, the serried cemeteries where the arrows of fate begin; even as Mourad, Nedjma, Rachid, and I; our ruined tribe refuses to change color; we have always married each other; incest is our bond, our principle of cohesion since the first ancestor's exile; the same blood irresistibly bears us to the delta of the passional stream, near the siren who drowns all her suitors rather than choose among the sons of her tribe—Nedjma concluding her stratagem, a queen fugitive and without hope until the husband's appearance, the black man forearmed against the social incest, and this at last will be the nation's tree taking root in the tribal sepulcher, under the cloud, pierced at last, of a blood too often skimmed . . .

NEDJMA | pp. 247–250.


Lakhdar and Mustapha leave the club to look for pennants.
The farmers are ready for the parade.
"Why the devil have they brought their cattle?"
Field workers, factory workers, businessmen. Sun. A big crowd.
*Germany has surrendered.*
Couples. Bars crowded.
The bells.
Official ceremony: monument to the dead.
The police keep their distance.
*Popular counter-demonstration.*
Enough promises. 1870. 1918. 1945.
Today, May 8, is it victory this time?
The scouts march past first, then the students.
Lakhdar and Mustapha march side by side.
The crowd swells.
Four abreast.
No one in the streets can resist the pennants.
The Cadres are broken.
The anthem begins on the children's lips:
*De nos montagnes s'élève*

*La voix des hommes libres.*

Mustapha sees himself at the heart of an impregnable centipede.

With the strength of so many mustaches, so many hard feet, they can stare down the *colons*, the police, the fleeing rabble.

A member of the secret police, hidden in the shadow of an arcade, shoots at the flag.

*Machine-guns.*

The Cadres dissolve.

They have let the demonstrators be disarmed at the mosque by the commissioner, with the mufti's help.

Chairs.

Bottles.

Branches cut on the way.

The Cadres are vanquished.

*Defeat the people in their first mass demonstration?*

The standard-bearer collapses.

A former combatant seizes his bugle.

Reveille or Holy War?

With his sword a farmer slices open the shoulder of a student whose short hair makes him look like a European.

Mustapha throws away his tie.

The French mayor is struck down by a policeman.

A restaurant-owner rolls in his reddened burnoose.

*Lakhdar and Mustapha are separated in the confusion.*

There are only three students left around Mustapha; an old Jewess throws her flowerpot at one of them, more to get it off her window-sill than to hit anyone . . .

NEDJMA|pp. 304–305.

REFERENCES

Serreau, Geneviève. "Situation de l'écrivain algérien. Interview de Kateb Yacine," *Les Lettres Nouvelles*, July–August, 1956, pp. 107–112.

Glissant, Edouard. "Le Chant profond de Kateb Yacine," *Les Lettres Nouvelles*, January, 1959, pp. 7–9.

Serreau, Geneviève. "Kateb Yacine," *Les Lettres Nouvelles*, April 29, 1959, pp. 8–10.

Joyaux, Georges J. "Driss Chraïbi, Mohammed Dib, Kateb Yacine, and Indigenous North African Literature," *Yale French Studies*, 24 (Summer, 1959), pp. 30–40.

Meade, Claude Y. "Nedjma: roman nord-africain de langue française," *The French Review*, December, 1960, pp. 146–151.

## A NOTE ON THE TYPE

THE TEXT of this book was set on the Linotype in
BODONI BOOK, a printing type so called after Giam-
battista Bodoni (1740–1813), a celebrated printer and
type designer of Rome and Parma. Bodoni Book as
produced by the Linotype company is not a copy of
any one of Bodoni's fonts, but is a composite, modern
version of the Bodoni manner. Bodoni's innovations
in printing-type style were a greater degree of contrast in the "thick and thin" elements of the letters
and a sharper and more angular finish of details.

---

*Composed, printed, and bound by*
*Kingsport Press, Inc., Kingsport, Tennessee.*
*Typography and binding design by*
MAXINE SCHEIN